THE SECOND MRS HARDY

the printer's hands. The
second part is at present
chaos, but I shall be able
to get that in order later.

Strange complications
seem to come into my life
and unreal situations. I
often wonder where I am
drifting — or why. Some
time later I should so like
to have a talk with you.

On the 21st. I go to

Letter from Florence Hardy to Siegfried Sassoon

The
Second Mrs Hardy

by

ROBERT GITTINGS

and

JO MANTON

HEINEMANN
LONDON

UNIVERSITY OF WASHINGTON PRESS
SEATTLE

Heinemann Educational Books Ltd
22 Bedford Square, London WC1B 3HH
LONDON EDINBURGH MELBOURNE AUCKLAND
HONG KONG SINGAPORE KUALA LUMPUR NEW DELHI
IBADAN LUSAKA NAIROBI JOHANNESBURG
KINGSTON PORT OF SPAIN

British Library CIP Data
Gittings, Robert
  The Second Mrs Hardy.
  1. Hardy, Thomas, b. 1840 – Relationship with women.
  2. Hardy, Florence Emily   3. Novelists, English –
  19th century – Wives
  I. Title   II. Manton, Jo
  823'.8   PR4753

  ISBN 0–435–18366–4

Library of Congress Catalog Card Number 79–63567
ISBN 0–295–95668–2 (U.S.)

Printed and bound in Great Britain by
Butler & Tanner Ltd, Frome and London

To James Gibson
Hardy scholar and friend

Contents

List of Illustrations viii

Acknowledgements ix

Introduction: *Cakes and Ale* 1

PART I: FLORENCE DUGDALE

1 "Quiet, Humble and Obedient" 9

2 "The Drudgery of Teaching" 16

3 "I Love Writing" 24

4 "A Scribbling Woman" 30

5 "Dear, Kind Friends" 38

6 "Times Not Easy" 46

7 "Mute Ministrations" 55

8 "From Youth to Dreary Middle-Age" 65

PART II: FLORENCE HARDY

9 "If My Name Were Gifford" 77

10 "A Tremendous Job in Hand" 84

11 "Regarded and Treated as Hostess" 91

12 "Things That One Cannot Write About' 99

13 "So Futile and Hopeless" 107

14 "Time and Her Friends" 113

15 "Coin of Another Realm" 122

16 "What Life Was" 129

Abbreviations used in Notes 136

Notes 137

Short List of Printed Sources 145

Index 146

Illustrations

Frontispiece   Letter from Florence Hardy to Siegfried Sasson

1.	Florence Dugdale aged about 20	17
2.	St. Andrew's Church of England School, Enfield: (a) Edward Dugdale, Headmaster; (b) Prebendary Hodson, Chairman of managers; (c) Standard Four in 1897	20
3.	Florence Dugdale in her twenties	31
4.	Sir Thornley Stoker	41
5.	Florence Dugdale aged about 30	44
6.	Thomas Hardy at 69, painted by his sister Mary	48
7.	Florence and Hardy on Aldeburgh beach, taken by an amateur photographer on 16 August 1909	50
8.	Florence at Max Gate drawn by William Strang, 26 September 1910	58
9.	Two employers: (a) Emma Hardy in old age; (b) Florence Henniker outside 13 Stratford Place	62
10.	Florence with "Wessex" at Max Gate soon after her marriage	78
11.	Hardy and Florence in their garden, about 1920	89
12.	H. G. Wells and Rebecca West visit the Hardys, 1919	94
13.	Hardy aged 86, drawn by Alfred Wollmark, 5 July 1926	105
14.	Sir James Barrie at the unveiling of the Hardy Memorial, 2 September 1931	119
15.	Florence in the last year of her life	124
16.	The drawing-room at Max Gate, in which Florence died	130

Reproduced by permission of the Dorset County Museum, except for 2, 4, 12, 13, which are by permission of the London Borough of Enfield, the Wellcome Trustees, Dame Rebecca West, D.B.E. and Macmillan (London), and the University of London Periodicals Library respectively. Frontispiece by permission of the Provost and Fellows of Eton College.

Acknowledgements

A FULLY-DOCUMENTED biography of Florence Hardy could never have been written without the help of many informed and enthusiastic people; it is a pleasure to record how much the joint authors owe to them.

The first thirty-five years of the life of Florence Dugdale, before she became Thomas Hardy's second wife, were spent largely in Enfield. There, Dr. Graham Handley, Principal Lecturer in English at the College of All Saints, Tottenham, made extensive local enquiries and personal research. Sylvia Collicot generously made her own researches on the School Board of Enfield available. Peter Glennie, present headmaster of St. Andrew's Church of England Primary School, allowed us to read the school's early log-books. J. Westaway, M.B.E., and L. Davies contributed recollections of their own schooldays. Mrs W. A. Prince, secretary of St. Andrew's church, verified information from the parish registers. David Pam, Local History and Museums Officer, gave valuable advice on local sources.

Further light was thrown on Florence Dugdale's early years by information from a number of people. The Secretariat of the British Museum supplied information about her Reader's ticket. Professor Michael Millgate listed the dates of Hardy's still-unpublished letters to her. Mrs. A. MacCaw gave personal information about her own grandfather Bram Stoker and the Stoker family of Dublin. Dr. M. Roberts contributed information on the Dugdale and Hyatt families. Mrs. and Miss Gibberd supplied information about the boyhood of Alan Gibberd, to whom Florence Dugdale dedicated her best children's book.

Information about Florence Hardy's life in Dorchester was kindly supplied by Dr. Romana Bartellot, Mrs. Gertrude Bugler, M. A. Edwards, R. Fare, J.P., and Miss E. Margaret Lane. Hardy experts consulted by us included James Gibson, as always a ready source, Miss Evelyn Hardy, Dr. Desmond Hawkins, Denys Kay-Robinson, F. B. Pinion; Alan Clodd generously lent the diary of his grandfather Edward Clodd, Hardy's exact contemporary and friend; Dr. John Fines supplied specialized information on pupil-teacher training, and Professor E. Sampson encouraged us to draw on his work on Hardy and Mrs. Hardy as magistrates. Peter Coxon communicated the contents of unpublished letters at the University of St. Andrews.

Librarians, archivists, and curators who, with their staffs, have given invaluable help include Kenneth Carter of the Dorset County Library, Miss M. Holmes of the Dorset County Record Office, Michael Meredith of the Eton School Library, and R. N. R. Peers of the Dorset County Museum.

The following acknowledgements are made to the owners of these documents: the British Library for Florence Hardy's letters to Marie Stopes and for Thomas Hardy's letters to Edward Clodd; the Brotherton Collection, the Brotherton Library, the University of Leeds, for letters from Florence Hardy to Edward Clodd and from Edward Clodd to Clement Shorter; the Director, Special Collections, Colby College, Waterville, Maine, for letters from Florence Hardy to Paul Lemperly and to Rebecca Owen; the Trustees of the Thomas Hardy Collection and the Curator of the Dorset County Museum for the typescript of James Barrie's letters to Florence Hardy and for Florence Hardy's letters to Emma Hardy; the Dorset County Record Office for letters from Florence Hardy to the Vicar and churchwardens of Stinsford, for the Dorset County Hospital annual reports and the Borough of Dorchester Petty Sessions Minute Books; the Provost and Fellows of Eton College for Florence Hardy's letters to Louisa Yearsley and Siegfried Sassoon, and for Kate Hardy's postcard collection; the Fawcett Society for Emma Hardy's letters to the London Society for Women's Suffrage; M. A. Edwards and the Mill Street Housing Society for the Society's Minutes; Lock Collection, Dorset County Library, for Kate Hardy's Diary; H. P. R. Hoare and the National Trust for Florence Hardy's letters to Alda, Lady Hoare in the Wiltshire County Record Office. The Trustees of the late E. A. Dugdale are thanked especially for their helpful acquiescence in our use of non-substantial quotation throughout the book from the letters of Florence Hardy. The sources of all these manuscripts and typescript documents are not further indicated.

Copyright in illustrations belongs to the Thomas Hardy Collection, Dorset County Museum, with the following exceptions: 2, the London Borough of Enfield; 4, the Wellcome Trustees; 12, Dame Rebecca West, D.B.E. and Macmillan (London); 13, University of London Periodicals Library; frontispiece, the Provost and Fellows of Eton College.

Introduction: *Cakes and Ale*

IN THE SUMMER of 1930 the ashes of Thomas Hardy had lain for two and a half years in Westminster Abbey. His comparatively young widow, Florence Emily Hardy, found herself at the centre of the great writer's cult. In their house, Max Gate, Dorchester, where she had shared Hardy's life for nearly twenty years, she received visits from literary researchers, or pilgrims who came to see where his heart was buried, beside his first wife and his kinsfolk in the quiet churchyard at Stinsford. Florence Hardy received these visitors kindly, especially perhaps those American academics who were planning learned studies of her husband's work. She herself had brought out, in the years since her husband's death, a two-volume biography and was therefore a source of authoritative information. Visitors were shown the study where many of the novels and poems had been written, and allowed to hear personal memories of the great man. Favoured researchers were invited to stay in the house. Moreover, Mrs. Hardy controlled, with a fellow-trustee, all the author's copyrights, which she herself owned.

The shock of losing her eighty-seven-year-old husband, so long the centre of her life, was severe. She attended the Abbey funeral accompanied by her own doctor, and a previous family doctor also offered his support. Perhaps because of her distress, misunderstandings had arisen from the start about a fitting memorial for Hardy. Well-meaning friends made conflicting proposals and the Hardy family were at odds with her co-trustee. The vicar and church-wardens of Stinsford therefore planned a first, modest memorial, a new stained-glass window in the village church. Florence Hardy naturally subscribed to the window[1] and was in due course invited to unveil it. She would have done so, but for one disturbing fact. This was the announcement of a novel by Somerset Maugham entitled *Cakes and Ale*, to be published in September 1930. Mrs. Hardy read that this dealt with a great writer, whose second wife did very well out of his reputation before and after death. Since Maugham barely knew the Hardys, he could not well portray their inner thoughts and feelings; nevertheless, the choice of subject seemed ominous.

Mrs. Hardy's alarm at the advertisements increased during October 1930, as the reviews came out. It appeared that the book's fictitious subject, Edward Driffield, like the late Thomas Hardy, was born and bred in the country, in humble circumstances, waited many years for recognition, had one of his best novels condemned and banned on station bookstalls, married a conspicuously devoted second wife, received the O.M., and returned to his birthplace to be a Grand Old Man. His novels, like Hardy's, were full of comic and Shakespearian "yokels". As J. B. Priestley wrote for American readers: "If Maugham did not intend his readers to be reminded of Hardy, then he acted with strange stupidity, (and a less stupid man than Somerset Maugham never set pen to paper)."[2] Priestley cheerfully "anticipated a colossal row". Other reviewers made it clear that the figure of the second wife was etched with biting malice. The reader learnt that this woman had married a great writer late in his life and "succeeded in making him respectable by degrees". His formerly Bohemian country household was "perfectly got up with the second Mrs. Driffield as stage manager".[3] This point was stressed in successive reviews; "the attempt of Driffield's dreary second wife to turn the hearty old rogue into a respectable Grand Old Man of English Letters provides excellent comedy". Reviewers appeared to share Maugham's contempt for "the humbug and non-sense which is talked about established literary reputations",[4] in which "respectable asses can always prevail over the truth".[5] Mrs. H. M. Tomlinson, attempting to defend the Hardys, made matters worse by assuming Maugham *must* have visited Max Gate. "Hospitality has seldom been so maltreated."[6] Most disquietingly of all for Hardy's widow, the plot of *Cakes and Ale* hinged upon a literary deception, a biography contrived by Driffield's widow to conceal the great man's rough past. Florence knew, as the general public did not, that her own official *Life*[7] of Hardy had in fact been composed by Thomas Hardy himself, carefully written in the third person, from sources which he then destroyed.

Florence Hardy read the reviews with understandable and extreme distress. She was now fifty-one and extremely sensitive. As a girl she had been brought up in an atmosphere of strict respectability, while as a woman she had lived for many years with Hardy's intense hatred of publicity. Always diffident, she now took advice from friends in London whose social experience would fit them to judge her position, in particular the daughter of Hardy's old friend, Lady Jeune, "always a very safe guide". On their advice, she wrote in October to the vicar of Stinsford declining to unveil the memorial window herself. "In a recent novel some very bitter things are said of a wife who 'exploits her husband's fame before and after death', and the reviewers have taken this to be aimed at myself, though the author strongly denies that."[8] To the churchwarden she wrote of "a barely-veiled attack on me in a recently published novel" and feared that "to unveil the window might give colour to that accusation". Instead she proposed Lady Ilchester, of the Wessex aristocracy, "a most kind friend to my husband from her girlhood—& also to myself". She added rather pathetically, "I have always tried to keep in the background as much as possible."[9] She was present, but took no active part in the unveiling ceremony.[10]

As these letters reveal, Mrs. Hardy had now read *Cakes and Ale* for herself, and considered it an "attack on me". In it she found the jealously-guarded privacy of her marriage invaded and held up to ridicule. She knew very well that in character she was nothing like the brisk, domineering Mrs. Driffield of the novel; for, as the observant young daughter of the rector of Fordington noticed, the second Mrs. Hardy, while talking to one politely, always seemed to be listening anxiously for complaints or sounds of domestic disaster in the background.[11] Far from "managing", she deferred to her famous husband. She had early lost her faith and substituted it for what Henry James called "genius worship". She had married Hardy, forty years older than herself, "that I might have the right to express my devotion and to endeavour to add to his comfort and happiness".[12] At whatever cost to her own health or happiness, she had gone on year after year, housekeeping, typing, answering the flood of letters she came to dread, reading aloud, barring the door to unwelcome visitors. Without this sacrificial devotion, many of Hardy's finest late poems might not have been written.

Yet, if the inner character was a travesty, the outer circumstances of her life had been observed with precise, sharp malice. Even her widowhood was not spared. Mrs. Driffield, with her husband dead and her occupation gone, is "awfully lonely". Florence had written to Siegfried Sassoon, "I still feel my life to be intolerably and unalterably lonely."[13] Mrs. Driffield had "been in the habit of making notes of Driffield's talk for years", because she planned a biography which would conceal Driffield's humble origins. Florence, towards the end of Hardy's life, had made notes of his early memories, and in 1927 had kept a diary recording his conversations. Like herself, Mrs. Driffield had originally been described as Driffield's secretary, but then became, like Florence's own sister who nursed Hardy on his death-bed, a hospital nurse. The house, Max Gate, which Maugham had never visited, was the subject of witty ridicule. Florence had struggled for years to run it as Hardy wanted it, though with increasing difficulty. His original villa of 1885 might have been manageable,[14] but the extensions of 1898 and 1908, false turrets, attics, outbuildings, back kitchen and three long stone passages, were a nightmare to a delicate and easily-tired housekeeper. Florence had suffered from Hardy's refusal to allow anything to be altered.[15] She had tried to persuade him to move, "but he simply *won't*". Over the years she had gradually, tactfully arranged the house to her own liking with fresh chintzes, Chippendale furniture collected by Hardy, silver-framed photographs and rosebowls.[16] *Cakes and Ale* ridiculed this décor, in "what can only be described as the acme of good taste". Maugham described in cruel detail rooms so conventional "that it was slightly disconcerting". The great author's study, in particular, was a scene "perfectly set. I do not know why the room seemed so strangely dead; it had already the mustiness of a museum." This was the more painful because Florence had learnt her standards of taste, long before her marriage, from a much-loved friend who had since died. Her most intimate campaigns, to install a bathroom[17] which Hardy declined to use, or to wean him from his favourite study trousers mended with packing thread,[18] had not gone unobserved. Mrs. Driffield "had to use a good deal of tact to get him to behave decently"; she observes her husband with little satisfied nods when his looks and manners conform to a higher social class.

The relations of the Driffield household with the outside world and Mrs. Driffield's social pretensions are gleefully described. Mrs. Driffield disposed in short order of "interviewers and authors who want him to read their books, and silly hysterical women". However, his county hostess confidently takes the narrator of *Cakes and Ale* to luncheon with the great author because, "Naturally we're different." Here Florence was vulnerable, for her weakness, shared with many of her contemporaries, was a Henry Jamesian love-affair with the upper classes. She asked Lady Hoare of Stourhead to bring her house-guests to visit Max Gate in the exact words, "different from anyone else in Wessex ... All your friends are welcome for your sake."[19] Yet on the same day, Florence complained, "*callers* are the bane of my life. The local clergy are the greatest sinners. They want to make T. H. a spectacle for the amusement of any friends who may be visiting them."[20] She noted, "some wretched strangers are coming and I must inspect them first to see they are not interviewers".[21] Florence's invariable kindness during her widowhood to American scholars was travestied in Mrs. Driffield's mercenary opportunism. She welcomes two professors, "'Americans?' said Mrs. Driffield. 'Say I shall be very pleased if they'll come in'", and shows them the great writer's study "with astonishing alacrity".

Florence could well feel herself personally caricatured by the book. In a particularly cruel aside, the second Mrs. Driffield was described as "not quite, quite a lady", a suggestion calculated to catch the second Mrs. Hardy on the raw. "For myself, I really do not care a hang whether people think I was a typist or not," she protested, but plainly, she did care.[22] As a young woman, Florence had a fragile beauty which continued to haunt Thomas Hardy for years. With middle age, ill-health and "the strain of keeping on, day after day, year in, year out", this beauty faded, as she was unhappily aware. When photographs came, "I considered them calmly—as I would the photographs of a stranger—I am bound to confess that I have no claims at all to anything approaching good looks." Modern fashions did not suit her and a new hat, "bare and rather severe", emphasized "my sallow complexion".[23] It was painful to read of Mrs. Driffield as "a woman of about five and forty . . . with a small sallow face and neat sharp features. She had a black cloche hat pressed tight down on her head."

Whatever the opinion of subsequent scholars, there was no doubt in Florence's mind that she and Hardy, their home and their social status, were maliciously portrayed in *Cakes and Ale*. More painful than any exterior description was Maugham's judgment of the great writer's character. "I think that when he had exhausted an emotion he took no further interest in the person who had aroused it. I should say that he had a peculiar combination of strong feeling and extreme callousness." Florence saw her life's work exposed to the pity or ridicule of strangers. No wonder this quiet, repressed woman felt, by November 1930, with the book read, "There are moments when I want to shake my fists at the sky, or shriek aloud in rage."[24]

She must have asked herself, and any reader must ask, how could such a thing have happened to her? Partly, perhaps, it was because she was so little known as an independent human being. Practically nothing has so far been written about her until the age of thirty-five, when she became the wife of Thomas Hardy and priestess of his cult. Visitors who praised her, as many did, for sacrificial devotion, seem to have cared little to ask about her as a human being in her own right. What information reached the world was carefully edited, either by Hardy or herself, sometimes with misleading effect. Yet Florence Dugdale, who became Florence Hardy, was an interesting figure, typical of her time and place, whose struggles have a pathos and irony not unworthy of Hardy himself. What was the real character of the second Mrs. Hardy?

Part I
Florence Dugdale

1

"Quiet, Humble and Obedient"

I N 1873 the poet Matthew Arnold, in his alternative career as Her Majesty's Inspector of Schools, visited St. Andrew's National School for Boys at Enfield, ten miles north of London. He found a school-house in cramped and churchy style, like those built by the poet Thomas Hardy in his alternative career as a "Gothic architect". A hundred and sixty boys sat on benches, "dame school fashion", in one room. Arnold found less "life and vigour" in such Church of England schools than in Dissenting schools. They seemed, he remarked shrewdly, "created for the class that is to use them by people above it";[1] but he wished the young headmaster well. The most surprising thing about this school was, in fact, the head-master's age and his future destiny. For Edward Dugdale was a headmaster at twenty-three, and forty years later was to become, to his own and everyone else's surprise, father-in-law of the seventy-four-year-old Thomas Hardy, O.M.

Mr. Dugdale had already travelled far from his birth in a crowded back-street just east of the Portsmouth Dockyard, where his father, William Dugdale, a blacksmith from Wareham, Dorset, lived among sailors, riggers, ferrymen, tide-waiters, ships' carpenters and dock-yard labourers. His mother, Emily Hibbs, was the daughter of a carter at Langton Matravers and both parents had come by sea to the little colony of Dorset families, driven from home to seek work in the port.[2] Edward, one of four boys, went by way of apprentice-ship as a pupil-teacher in Portsmouth to St. John's College, Batter-sea, run by the National Society "for Promoting the Education of the Poor in the Principles of the Established Church". He emerged in 1871 with the coveted parchment of a certificated teacher. The Education Act of 1870 demanded schools in every town and village; training colleges could hardly supply the demands of managers for at least a thousand new teachers. Anglicans especially were deter-mined to compete with the new board schools. The vicar of Enfield interviewed the brisk young teacher from Portsmouth and offered him the headship of his church school at once. Edward Dugdale seized the chance which historical accident had given him; he accepted the post and stayed as head of St. Andrew's National School for Boys for forty-seven years.

The salary was about a hundred and twenty pounds a year, riches to his Dorset ancestors and enough for the most responsible young man to consider marriage. He soon met a fellow church-worker a year older than himself, Emma Taylor, who had been born at the butcher's shop owned by her family for more than a hundred years. She worked as private governess to Miss Gwendolen Somerset at Enfield Court, was gentle, conscientious, musical and "very refined". Her parents died, so Emma and her sister Alicia went to live with an aunt at Brighton, but Edward, a forceful character, visited her there. They were married during the summer holidays of 1876 at St. Peter's Church, Brighton, overlooking the Steyne.[3] Their first daughter, Ethel, was born at Enfield in May 1877. By 1879 the school had outgrown its old buildings and moved to a new site. The Dugdales rented one of the semi-detached houses in the same street, and here, at 4 Hampton Villas, Sydney Road, their second daughter was born on 12 January 1879. She was christened, like many late-Victorian girls, Florence after Miss Nightingale and also Emily after her Dorset grandmother. Three more daughters followed: Constance in 1884, Eva in 1887 and Margaret in 1893.[4]

At five years old Florence began to attend the National Infants' School, under the headmistress Miss Butcher. For the next formative twenty-four years, until she finally left teaching in 1908, the various schools attached to St. Andrew's Church filled her life. Since her father and two sisters taught in the same schools, the ethos of the National Society pervaded the family; Florence was set from childhood on a course of duty, submission to authority and acceptance of the social order. The Education Act, in an attempt to satisfy conflicting interests, had left the old voluntary schools and the new board schools to compete for public support. Both could charge a few pence a week and received government grants; but where board schools had a guaranteed income "on the rates", church schools had to rely on unpredictable gifts or subscriptions. Inevitably they suffered shortages of trained teachers, buildings and materials. A kindly inspector found the National Infants' Schools "hardly places for infants to spend a happy day". Kindergarten bricks, paints, beads or sand were considered an unnecessary luxury for five-year-olds. Instead, Florence in 1884 had to "explain the Creed or give examples of the Commandments" in a scripture examination by the vicar. The benches, reported an H.M.I., were uncomfortable for small children, there were no tables or desks, the lavatory roof leaked and "ringworm still prevails". On a school treat the infants "went to Church and were addressed by the Vicar, then into the Park and back to School for tea". Yet the same inspector found the headmistress kind and intelligent, and in these bleak surroundings the children were well taught. At five Florence could perform the action song "Bread Making". At six she could read "The Kitten at Play".

At seven she learnt each week a suitable scripture verse, such as "Children, obey your parents", and a hymn by heart. She knew the stories of Abraham and Isaac, David and Goliath and the infant Samuel. In the afternoons she learnt needlework with the other little girls, while the boys were able to enjoy drawing. And, first intro-duction to English literature, she could recite Wordsworth's "We are Seven".[5]

At seven years Florence moved on to St. Andrew's Girls' School. This consisted of two rooms, one forty-eight feet by thirty-one, the other twenty-five by seventeen and a half. Here the headmistress and one assistant, with two pupil-teachers, had to teach 104 child-ren, a number which grew steadily with the growth of the town. Not surprisingly, epidemics were frequent; "measels", as the head-mistress always spelt it, left some pupils very depressed and with "bad eyes". In 1889 one little girl died of diphtheria. Yet somehow the children were taught and it is possible to trace Florence's early lessons year by year. At eight she was reading fluently from the National Readers, at nine writing and working sums on her slate; at ten she "commenced learning the poetry for the Government Exa-minations". At eleven she began geography from wall maps in which red showed the far-flung British Empire.[6] Every day began with a forty-minute scripture lesson in which chapters of the Bible were learnt by heart. Indeed, all learning was by rote. "The teacher has taken pains," wrote an inspector after his visit, "but she should try to get the girls to think more for themselves."[7] It was not a train-ing in independence of mind.

At home the Dugdale family grew. With remarkable enterprise Mr. Edward Dugdale had founded in 1880 the Enfield Independent Building Society, offering "prompt and liberal advances on easy terms of repayment". About 1890, with its aid, he himself became a house-owner at 5 River Front, Southbury Road, Enfield. This row of red-brick, semi-detached villas, with parlour bay-window to the front and narrow strip of garden to the rear, was the soul of respect-ability, and Mrs. Dugdale made it a happy home. A maid who lived with the family remembered them as nice people, affectionate and generous.[8] They were united against the world in a close family loyalty. Edward Dugdale, by hard work and discipline, had made the classic Victorian transition across class to gentility. The rough country past seemed buried and forgotten. "There are Dugdales at Wareham," wrote his daughter Florence in middle age, "but as far as I know, not the least relation to me."[9]

Edward Dugdale became by force of character a leading figure in the life of the town. A staunch Conservative, he helped to found the Enfield Town Constitutional Club. He was on the Committee of the Church of England Temperance Society, and compelled senior boys at his school to attend weekly anti-drinking meetings. He served as treasurer to the Philanthropic Institution, which before the days of national insurance came to the help of the sick or aged. He was known as a disciplinarian at home and at school. He saw his duty as a church school headmaster to teach church doctrine, with no room for doubt or question, and to enforce duty in daily life. The core of his character was a total, rigid religious faith.[10]

This eminently Victorian figure dominated Florence's early life. His chief pleasure was walking; handsome and vigorous, he strode out into the countryside, with her beside him, leading the first of several contentious fox-terriers, always a favourite breed with the Dugdale sisters. In the 1880s Palmers Green, Winchmore Hill and Southgate were still hamlets nestling in a tangle of lanes with bridle-paths, water splashes and green clearings where gipsy caravans parked.[11] On these walks, he fed her imagination with tales of a vanished past. As a small boy in Portsmouth he had talked to an old sailor who claimed to have fought with Nelson at the Battle of the Nile. As a student he was one of those chosen to take up a collection for the wounded of the Franco-Prussian war at a Red Cross service in Westminster Abbey; he described the heap of golden sovereigns, more money than he had ever seen in his life, on the collection plate. When little more than a boy, he had thrice rescued people from drowning in Portsmouth harbour. When Florence was fifteen he rescued a little girl from the New River and a few years later one of his own pupils who had fallen into a pond in the town park. He received a certificate from the Royal Humane Society.[12]

Another shaping influence was the town itself. Enfield, in the days when Keats went to school there, had been a country town with a fine fifteenth-century church, a Tudor grammar school, and the remains of a manor house with a magnificent cedar of Lebanon. It was surrounded by the parks of country seats, Forty Hall, Myddle-ton House and Enfield Court as well as the open Chase. The clear New River flowed through the parish from north to south, carrying London's drinking water. In 1849 came the railway, and Keats's old school was converted to form Enfield Town Station. During the Crimean War, the Royal Small Arms Factory at Enfield Lock switched to mass production methods.[13] Later growth brought four acres of workshops, streets of workers' houses, mission halls and "iron churches", police stations, workhouse schools and a fever hospital. The farms and fields, the wooded hamlets round old Enfield, slowly vanished under suburban streets. When Florence was fifteen, the whole area became an Urban District Council; the population, which had been under twenty thousand at her birth, rose to over fifty-six thousand by 1910.[14] The Dugdales lived opposite the Town Station and trams passed their door. Yet, decisively for the sensitive schoolgirl, the old Enfield still existed, in green paths, Church Walk, Holly Walk, the shady tow-path along the New River, the over-grown churchyard and the park with its lake. In dignified Gentle-mans' Row, Queen Anne houses sheltered in gardens where old fruit trees looked over the walls. They were still in Florence's memory when she came to write *In Lucy's Garden* in 1912. Her mother con-tributed accounts of Clayesmore and Enfield Court and the young gentlewomen there, to whom she had been governess.[15] Florence grew into a girl with a hunger for beauty, elegance and cultured society. The quest for them was to shape her life. She became a romantic, for whom fact and fantasy blurred. In middle age she told a visitor who noticed her "faint touch of sadness" that "she had had a lonely childhood, lacking affection".[16] She may have felt this sometimes, but all the objective evidence points in the opposite direction.

At twelve Florence reached the legal school-leaving age. There were high schools for girls in Enfield by the 1890s, including one where the headmistress had a Cambridge mathematics degree; but their average fees were six guineas a term,[17] and county scholar-ships, which might have helped an intelligent student, still lay ten years in the future. So in 1891 Florence followed her elder sister to the new Higher Grade school at a cost of ninepence a week. Higher Grade schools were elementary schools for pupils who did not want to go out to work at the earliest opportunity. Florence stayed here until fifteen, and according to a class-mate, attended no other school.[18] Her interest early fastened upon literature. At thirteen she read the works of Jane Austen, and was bitterly disappointed because, in spite of all she had heard about their excellence, they seemed to mean little to her. She wept over Paul Dombey's death, though, always found "glamour" in R. L. Stevenson and confessed to "a *great* weakness" for the society novels of Rhoda Broughton and Ouida. Already reading offered an escape to a grander, more exciting world.[19]

Emancipation for women, like education for the poor, was grudg-ingly doled out. Florence always knew that she and her sisters would have to earn their own livings, though later it seemed to her unfair that other girls need not.[20] She was growing up in the age of the New Woman, when in theory bicycles, tennis clubs, universities, the professions and the fight for the vote offered her freedom. In fact, the careers of elementary teachers and their families were confined to occupations which would support them while training. Florence's future appeared to be settled, like so many other girls of her back-ground, when she was fifteen. She had the essential qualifications to train as a teacher, good moral character and Standard Five of the Board of Education's Elementary Code. She began her years of pupil-teachership on 10 May 1895 at St. Andrew's Girls' School, where her elder sister Ethel was already apprenticed.[21] She was paid three shillings a week, rising to eight shillings in the final year; the bait was a Queen's Scholarship to the National Society's Training College at Tottenham. Of the sisters, Ethel became a teacher but married in the 1900s; Constance, also a teacher, stayed forty-six years at St. Andrew's Girls' School, retiring as headmistress in 1945. Eva went in 1908 to train as a nurse at Tottenham General Hospital[22] and devoted her life to nursing. The youngest sister trained as a teacher of domestic science and married during the war of 1914–18.[23] They were thus a typical family of their background and time. Florence was devoted to them all, but her solitary interest in literature seems to have set her a little apart.

Another lasting factor in her life soon emerged. Florence was not strong, and when exhausted was a prey to painful depression and self-doubt. The work of a pupil-teacher was very hard for girls scarcely out of childhood themselves and conditions in St. Andrew's Girls' School in the 1890s were harsh. The numbers had risen to 200, though in one epidemic of scarlet fever they fell as low as 127. Unable to afford the new building which was needed, the vicar and managers had bought a disused Wesleyan chapel and re-opened it on 15 June 1891 as "The Girls' National School".[24] In this tall, gloomy, un-heated vault three or even four classes were taught at the same time and the classes themselves were very large. It was useless for inspec-tors to recommend "teaching and training individual scholars as well as classes"; it was all the teachers could do to make themselves heard. Discipline had to be harsh; the log-books record in 1893 little girls caned for "insolence" and for being "insubordinate". An in-spector had already noted that "Ethel Dugdale seems constantly ill" and Florence was even less resistant; both sisters were frequently absent from "colds, influenza and sore throats".[25]

By the terms of her apprenticeship, Florence taught in this school for six hours a day; in return she was entitled to receive one and a half hour's tuition each day from the certificated head-teacher, Miss Dew. This had to be fitted in at eight in the morning and here Florence was fortunate, since some pupil-teachers started work as early as half-past six. Plans for an Enfield Pupil-Teachers' Centre by the Education Committee of the new district council were rejected on grounds of expense. Her whole life was governed by strict rules of conduct, and, as St. Andrew's was a church school, in addi-tion to blameless character, she needed a certificate from the vicar "that he was satisfied with her attention to her religious duties". At every school inspection, her work was examined by the visiting H.M.I., a fearful ordeal for a frightened girl. In school she was re-quired to be at all times "quiet, humble and obedient". Nassau

Senior called pupil-teachership "a system of the highest pressure. For seven years her mind is in a state of constant tension; she goes through struggle after struggle, in each of which a defeat is ruinous."[26] Florence was not built by nature to withstand this life.

The strain might have been endurable if the school itself were good, but there is evidence that at this time it was not. Successive inspectors had already complained of dangerous overcrowding, of the dismal schoolroom, "dark, inconvenient in shape and unheated" and of classes too large for teachers to control. Two headmistresses had left in rapid succession. "But even with all allowance for difficulties," wrote a not unsympathetic inspector, "I cannot speak favourably of the condition or the attainments." There was no understanding in the children's answers, spelling and writing were poor, arithmetic "bad and remarkably unintelligent".[27] At a later visit, he added regretfully, "I cannot say that any progress is visible." The curriculum was out of date and boring. Florence had a passion for reading and already showed gifts, which later pupils remembered, for telling stories to children. The school required her to teach needlework, tonic sol-fa, catechism by heart, with no explanations given, and "object lessons on Coal, Papers, Soap, Candles, Cocoa and Pins and Needles". Damningly, in 1896 the school was refused the higher grant given for efficiency.[28]

Ethel Dugdale, a girl of spirit left without permission when "rebuked" and refused to return. She finished her apprenticeship at her father's school across the road and won a Queen's Scholarship to training college at Tottenham. Florence was given leave of absence to study at home, but returned and struggled on alone. In June 1896, both sisters went to St. Martin's Hall, Charing Cross, to receive prizes from the Diocesan Board of Education. After careful coaching by their father, they had passed in the first class of the all-important Religious Knowledge Examination. Florence had also won a prize for "proficiency in secular subjects"; the prizes were handed to her by the Marchioness of Salisbury, a dazzling figure from the world of her favourite novels.[29] But the strain of the work told on her fragile health. In the winter of 1896–7, when her eighteenth birthday fell, she was six times absent through illness. On 5 March 1897 she "resigned her duties owing to ill-health", though she later completed the final two terms of her apprenticeship at the Pupil-Teachers central classes.[30] Her whole schooling had been dictated by people above her. Instead of the independence Matthew Arnold had hoped to see, girls in her position were taught an anxious compliance and devotion to duty. For better or worse these qualities marked Florence Dugdale's life.

2

"The Drudgery of Teaching"

AT EIGHTEEN came the first of many disappointments in Florence Dugdale's life, her failure to win the coveted Queen's Scholarship to training college. This was a highly competitive examination in which only one candidate in four succeeded and, although conscientious, Florence was fatally lacking in confidence. The alternative was to gain a teaching certificate under Article Fifty of the Education Code, which admitted candidates with a satisfactory record of four years' service as teacher to a qualifying examination. The decision was taken by 22 December 1897, when Mr. Dugdale wrote in his stout maroon School Log-Book, "Miss F. E. Dugdale to commence with Standard One on the 10th prox." On 10 January, two days before her nineteenth birthday, Florence, assisted by a monitor, began to teach the bottom form of her father's school, at the usual starting salary for women of eighty-five pounds a year.[1]

St. Andrew's Boys' School consisted of three red-brick class rooms in an asphalt playground, set below the level of Sydney Road. A high fence kept small boys in, but could not keep out noise from the railway or a neighbouring sawmill. The twenty-year-old buildings were already overcrowded. "The recognized accommodation of the school", wrote one of Her Majesty's Inspectors, "by no means corresponds to its real capacity. The room or section of a room in which Standard One is at present taught is so inconvenient and so ill-lighted as to be scarcely fit for use. Four of the classes are too large for the teachers in charge of them, nor with the existing staff (six out of seven teachers being uncertificated) can any re-organization be suggested."[2] Florence's gloomy class room contained eighty-eight little boys, many of them, as her father noted, the "waifs and castaways" of the town. The managers reluctantly agreed to put in two sliding glass partitions, still there fifty years later when the buildings were finally abandoned.[3]

The home background of many boys was bleak. In winter, when the weather was bad, some boys simply stayed at home; "want of boots and sickness real or imagined are the prevalent causes," wrote Edward Dugdale. One boy was sent home because his clothes were "so saturated with oil and dirt as to be offensive to those near him". The N.S.P.C.C. Inspector was called to investigate the case of a little boy who seemed persistently hungry, dirty and neglected. Mrs. Dugdale

1   Florence Dugdale aged about 20

was kind and generous to the poorer children; unobtrusively she collected second-hand boots and warm clothing for them, or sent hot meals to families in need.[4] There was nowhere in the school to dry wet clothing and in 1905 the borough surveyor complained of defective washrooms and water closets. The vicar counted each class personally to refute the charge of overcrowding,[5] but no amount of disinfectant could prevent epidemics in the crammed building. Scarlet fever and measles broke out in 1900, influenza every winter, diphtheria in 1904. "Measles and mumps still rife among children" and "much sickness in various classes", are typical entries. Mr. Dugdale was ill most winters himself with "influenza", which he always wrote in quotation marks as though he did not really believe in it. The effect of the school on Florence's frail health will appear in time.

Discipline was another anxiety, since here Florence felt she must not disappoint her much-loved father. Mr. Dugdale, though just, was a martinet, who ruled his little kingdom sternly. "Stick" played its part in his classes, and he was said to lead boys out to execution by the ear. When he was sent "a small leather strap by the Education Committee as an instrument of punishment, I sent it to the Girls' School, as more fitting to girls or infants than to boys".[6] Florence confessed indirectly, through a fictive persona, that she was "painfully lacking in strength" as a disciplinarian, "a fact many times impressed upon her by the headmaster". The teaching was necessarily as rigid as the discipline, since St. Andrew's had been until quite recently subject to the system of Payment by Results, a grant entirely dependent on a yearly examination of each child over six in reading, writing and arithmetic. This system produced teaching different, not merely in quantity but in kind, from the liberal education of the literate classes; it was, wrote Matthew Arnold, "a remedy worse than the disease it was supposed to cure".[7] Registration, revision, tests and "Standards" ruled the school day, year in, year out. "Went through with the teachers the weak points of the School Instruction," wrote conscientious Mr. Dugdale in October 1902. Next year, "an examination of 'Back Work' in Arithmetic shows the necessity of constant revision". In July at the end of the 1903 school year, "I finished an individual and exhaustive examination". Florence, sensitive and nervous, dreaded these interrogations. Yet now, as later in life, she suppressed her inner rebellion, submitting to duty, her father's stern Victorian god, with apparent compliance. Only in her early writings could she admit "the drudgery of teaching" or "the sum of the misery" she suffered in school.[8]

The subjects taught were laid down by the Board of Education Codes. In a typical school year, when Florence was twenty-six, geography was taught "with special reference to British Possessions", history by "twelve Lessons from the History Reader", English by

"Arnold and Jack's Series of Lessons, Grammar, Parsing, Analysis, Dictation as a means of testing Spelling", with "Remainder of Instruction as per Code".[9] "We went to school to learn," an old boy remembered, "even if it were only the three Rs, and woe betide us if we didn't learn ... We started on some particular subject on Monday morning and if we didn't know it by the end of the week, well we simply carried on during the next week until we did ... Arithmetic was drilled, day in day out and Copperplate writing, thin lines for the upstrokes, thick lines for the down, six words to a line and five minutes to write each line properly," a preparation for life as a clerk in an office.[10] Many years of this curriculum instilled into Florence an anxious, careful correctness, which was such a feature of her life and writing.

There is evidence that she taught well, from pupils of long ago, who nevertheless still remember her. "Her approach to us boys in class was a gentle one," wrote one old boy. "She had my brother in her class," wrote an Enfield resident. "He liked her very much and I think all the boys in her class thought a good deal of her. She was a very good teacher." She told stories to her six-year-olds and "could get people just to listen to her talk". She even wrote little plays for them to act. The children missed her if she were absent on sick-leave. Her first known autograph is a postcard from Worthing to her ink-monitor, which was posted during a spell of leave on 21 March 1905, and which said she would soon be back at school.[11] Though boys as a class are not susceptible to the charms of teachers, all agree that "Teacher Florrie", slender and serious, with gentle voice and large, luminous grey eyes, appealed to all but the toughest. The inspectors noticed her success. "The composition of the First Class deserves special commendation," wrote one H.M.I. in 1905. She managed to fit something of her own into the choice of "Recitations of extracts from classic English poets suitable for boys". In her first year as teacher, she taught seven-year-olds R. L. Stevenson's *Land of Story Books*; for older boys she suggested her favourite Tennyson, Arnold's *Forsaken Merman*, Gray's *Elegy*, Coleridge's *Ancient Mariner* and *The Ballad of Chevy Chase*. With other women teachers, she took the children for annual treats to the seaside or the London Zoo and weekly to the town park for "object lessons upon Nature". Later, as a children's writer, she came to specialize in nature study. The same H.M.I. praised her and her colleagues, in spite of all their material difficulties, for "earnest care for the children in their charge".[12]

It is clear that Florence was increasingly unhappy in her work. Her situation was typical of many teachers, trapped in the rivalry between state and voluntary schools. School board elections were still fought on sectarian grounds and National Schools imposed

(a) Edward Dugdale, Headmaster   (b) Prebendary Hodson, Chairman of managers

2 St. Andrew's Church of England School, Enfield

(c) Standard Four in 1897

particular constraints on the teacher. He or she could be dismissed by the managers "on grounds connected with the giving of religious instruction", without recourse to the local authority. The school provided boys and teachers to sing in the church choir, while the headmaster, his staff and family were expected to attend Sunday services regularly. On Empire Day, after the ceremony of saluting the flag, the vicar gave boys and staff "a stirring address on the meaning of Empire Day and their duties as citizens of a great Empire".[13] The vicar of Enfield, all-important in this little world, was a controversial figure. G. H. Hodson was an elderly bachelor, a classical scholar from Trinity College, Cambridge, a Prebendary of St. Paul's and brother of the distinguished Indian Army officer Hodson of Hodson's Horse, whose biography he wrote.[14] He was remote, austere and alarming; children were known to run away at the sight of the vicar's gaunt, black-clad figure. His devotion to the children of his parish was unquestionable, but his approach to their education was partisan in the extreme. "Dependence upon God and reliance upon His Holy Spirit" could only be taught in an Anglican school, and he denounced the new board schools as secular and godless. He, or his curate, visited St. Andrew's several times a week, to inspect children and staff alike. From 1894, when Enfield became a local authority, the vicar led a church and conservative pressure group in the new Education Committee. He refused as far as possible to offer free places or accept workhouse children in church schools, while attacking the "lavish" expenditure on teaching, light, space and playgrounds in board schools; this would of course prevent them from offering better conditions than National Schools. At a public meeting in 1895, Prebendary Hodson secured a resolution that "the limitation of expenditure of Board Schools by some superior authority is a matter of primary importance".[15] The liberal party on the council retaliated with attacks on the church schools for overcrowded and insanitary buildings, also for overworked and largely uncertificated teachers. Controversy filled the local press in the mid-1890s, and Florence Dugdale as a teacher knew that many of the criticisms were justified. Her father regarded her as "a Radical", to him a term of serious reproach.[16]

In spite of affection for her father and years of religious instruction, Florence came to dislike the clergy, the church and eventually all forms of belief. "Personally, I am without any religion," she wrote to a woman friend in later years. "It seems to me quite impossible for an intelligent person to believe in a beneficent deity."[17] This became one of the bonds between her and Thomas Hardy; "we both came to the conclusion that there was not a grain of evidence that the gospel story is true in any detail".[18] The roots of this agnosticism grew during her years as a church school teacher. Equally galling was the teacher's social subordination to the clergy and managers. Teachers were the first profession to graduate from the working classes by their own efforts, and social attitudes to them were condescending, until at least the end of the nineteenth century. "Pretensions such as the certificated teacher sometimes puts forth must be crushed and checked without mercy," wrote a correspondent of the *Quarterly Review* in the year of Florence's birth. A correspondent to *The Times* noted that teachers "are generally of so inferior a class that they do not venture to sit down in the presence of the clergyman". By comparison with the manager, the teacher was "a person of inferior manners and education".[19] Florence had been brought up by a careful mother to an ideal of "refinement", and continued to educate herself by quite wide reading. Distinction of birth, breeding or intellect held for her an almost magical charm and she saw herself, reasonably from her point of view, as "an educated gentlewoman". An early photograph shows her with white frock, shady straw hat and terrier on leash, a girl who would not have been out of place at any garden party, yet as a teacher she was not allowed to address a school manager directly. Florence grew acutely conscious of social distinctions and morbidly sensitive to slights.

As her twenties passed, there seemed little prospect of any other life than teaching. At twenty-seven she was given a week's leave of absence by the managers to take the Board of Education's Certificate Examination. Later she learnt that she had passed and was the holder of Teacher's Certificate No O6/4298, with special credit in English Literature, Composition and the Principles of Education.[20] This was and remained her only professional qualification as the writer she hoped to become. For the school it was important, since a certificated teacher earned a higher grant; as one of only two certificate holders, she was promoted to take the top class. Her father proudly wrote that she "has given lessons on the French Revolution to Standard Seven".[21] This meant she had to leave the small children she seems genuinely to have liked for a crowd of restless, bored twelve-year-olds, impatient to escape from the classroom.

Florence's chief trouble as a teacher was undoubtedly ill-health. Her mother was increasingly delicate in middle age, and also suffered from "mental depressions",[22] both handicaps which Florence inherited. She suffered from continual minor illnesses, colds, toothache, eyestrain and headaches. Mr. Dugdale, with his rigid code of justice, was most unlikely to favour his daughter at the expense of other members of his staff, but he was constantly forced to give Florence sick-leave. The major problem, from the first, was her throat. Before she had worked for a month, her father noted, "Miss F. E. Dugdale has lost her voice and is unable to attend school."[23] She was unable to teach, sometimes for several weeks, because of

an inflamed and painful throat. Tiredness or depression always made
it worse. "This is due to the system being run down, so that talking
exhausts and the throat becomes sore," explained her father in an
apologetic note to the managers.[24] Florence had attacks of laryngitis
severe enough to be recorded in January and February 1899, June
1902 and January 1903, when she was given a month's leave of
absence for general ill-health, with a further month in June of the
same year. In 1904 she was away in July and in September, wrote
her father, "was so ill that I forbade her attendance". A fortnight
later she was "very unwell again". In 1905 she was absent for the
whole of March with acute laryngitis, for which she went to Worthing, and in February 1906 was "unwell for some time past and absent
with pharyngitis". She returned, but in March had to be sent home
and was away for over a week. In December 1907 she attempted
to teach with a heavy cold and was ill for weeks with influenza. Her
monitor remembered her absences, and days when she seemed very
depressed.[25] This was surely hardly surprising.

A story about a young teacher which Florence began to write early
in 1907 reveals something of her unhappiness. Rows of boys fidget
and whisper through a hot, weary afternoon. They gabble their way
through Shelley's poem *To a Skylark*, "dull-eyed and uncomprehend-
ing". Their dirty clothes, their hob-nailed boots, their bovine faces,
the stuffy classroom, the other teachers, "eagerly discussing some
obscure point in the latest Code issued by the Board of Education",
all complete the young hero's wretchedness. For of course he has
"a love of poetry over-keen for an elementary school teacher"; he
hates "the drudgery of teaching" and "school life hems him round
like a prison".[26] This account, vivid and convincing enough, is the
only time Florence drew directly on her experiences as a teacher.
D. H. Lawrence, with similar experience, might bring the world
of the elementary school out of obscurity and turn its people's lives
to literature. Florence, it seems, preferred to forget the years in the
prison house, for she told a later acquaintance that life had given
her "very little opportunity to have much to do with children".[27]
Her obituary records that she "had been educated for the profession
of teaching, but ill-health did not permit her to take it up and she
turned instead to writing". Her father, correctly described as headmaster of a National School and member of a Dorset family, "was
numbered among the friends of Thomas Hardy, who took an interest
in the literary efforts of the second girl".[28] However ambiguously,
this stated an important truth. For Florence, however unfavourable
the circumstances, was determined to be a writer.

3

"I Love Writing"

THE WAKE of Queen Victoria's two Jubilees raised a wave of literary patriotism. The early 1900s were the age of the cheap edition, the series of reprinted classics, the selection of gems from, or half-hours with, great writers, the gift book in sage green or purple limp leather, of clubs devoted to Dickens, Browning or Tennyson. The author, once a seedy denizen of Grub Street, was metamorphosed into the English Man of Letters. Many young people, who would now be university students, were then struggling, with varying success, to educate themselves by reading. For many people the ideal of the literary life held a compelling magic and authority; for Florence Dugdale, it was the force which shaped her destiny.

"Personally," wrote Florence rather pathetically in middle age, "I simply *love* writing, poor though the result may be."[1] The dream of herself as a "literary woman" had existed since her pupil-teacher days. In that hard and narrow life, books became an escape and later, as faith faded, literature a substitute religion. During her many illnesses she read voraciously and her idea of the world was largely formed from books. In everyday life she was often uncertain, often surprised and hurt by events she might have foreseen.[2] The great social changes of the twentieth century, war, the rise of the labour movement, the emancipation of women, seemed to take her by surprise. Young women of her own age were already making their mark as physicians, social workers or journalists; thousands of all social classes marched to claim the vote for women. Florence remained strangely indifferent. When finally called on to take part in an election, she claimed to be "so vague that ... my head spins and I heartily wish women had never been given the vote".[3] Steeped in Victorian literature, she preferred to look towards a romantic past. "With regard to women," she wrote, "they are only strong when they realize their weakness and dependence upon men."[4] Not surprisingly, Florence's literary friends or patrons tended to be men, and men considerably older than herself.

In Enfield she early established herself as an aspiring writer. With her elder sister as chaperone, she attended the "conversaziones" of the Enfield Literary Union at the Bycullah Athenaeum, ornament of a select residential part of the town. Here Florence, so young, studious and serious, must have made a good impression, for in 1901

she was invited to deliver a paper. Given her training, the choice
of subject was almost inevitable. An examiner of pupil-teachers
remarked sadly that, whatever subjects were set for English papers,
"almost everybody chose the *Legend of Arthur*. The subject was evidently attractive, especially to female students." Like her fellow
teachers, Florence had evidently "diligently conned and committed
to memory" large chunks of Tennyson's *Idylls of the King*.[5] This
paper is the earliest evidence we have of her literary taste and style.

King Arthur, she told the assembled Literary Union, appeals
strongly to an inborn sense of romance. He is "the perfect knight
of the twenty-first century", a somewhat optimistic forecast. His
story is "beyond improvement" and the holy grail "an allegory of
the highest and most spiritual type". As for Lancelot and Elaine,
"there is no English love poem to equal it". Elaine, the lily maid,
is the embodiment of "pure and innocent love", contrasted with the
insidious "guilty love", tainted by sex, of Queen Guinevere. Elaine
"muses over each dint" in Lancelot's shield, her love "milder than
any mother with sick child". As for Lancelot, "his sin effectually
prevents him attaining the Grail". Arthur, by contrast, finds the
supreme revelation in fulfilling his aristocratic duty, a key concept
to Florence, as to most Victorian readers. "Of his last beautiful
speech from the barge, it is needless to speak; it is beyond praise."[6]
This was the dream world of the twenty-two-year-old teacher, soon
to be caught in a real life situation of the twentieth century.

Florence's chairman at this meeting "alluded in appreciative
terms to Miss Dugdale's literary qualifications". Against all the
odds, she had already begun to write, though her only outlet so far
had been the children's column of the local newspaper. She owed
this, and the most formative friendship of her life, to her first literary
mentor, A. H. Hyatt. His family were well known to Florence. Their
father had been an Enfield fishmonger near her grandfather's
butcher's shop, and two daughters had been monitors at her own
school. Elizabeth Hyatt came in 1902 to share the teaching of
Florence's pupils in Standard One. The solitary brother, Alfred
Hyatt, was ten years older than Florence and had been a pupil of
her father; his further education was hindered by a stammer so distressing that at times he could hardly be understood. He went to
work as store-keeper for a music publisher, Charles Sheard, at 192
High Holborn. Perhaps because of his speech handicap, he turned
to writing as a means of self-expression and from about 1895 began
to compose lyrics for the drawing-room ballads published by his
firm. He developed tuberculosis, and was forced to settle with his
widowed mother and sisters in what must have been a crowded small
house at 19 Palace Gardens, Enfield. Although an invalid, Hyatt
was of necessity a tireless freelance writer. He founded the Cedars

Press, which brought out small hand-printed editions and continued to publish *Lyrics in various Keys*.[7] He dressed "like a poet", in the cloak and broadbrimmed hat of Florence's favourite Tennyson, and she believed fervently that if he lived, he would become a great poet. His handicaps and his loneliness appealed to her protective tenderness; though he was too ill and too poor for any hope of marriage, he remained for her "the only person who ever loved me". By her own account, years later, this sad and tender love was the deepest relationship in Florence's life.[8]

Hyatt secured publication for Florence's earliest writings from 1899, when she was only twenty, by sharing with her his regular children's column in the *Enfield Observer*. For four or five years they wrote this jointly; it was a close collaboration on a theme chosen each week, for which Hyatt supplied verses and Florence a prose passage signed "Amita". Amita's identity was well known in the town and an Enfield resident remembers winning a competition prize from Florence in 1900.[9] The effects of this apprenticeship were lasting. Florence showed a genuine gift for writing in hasty letters to friends with whom she felt at ease. Then she was observant, amusing, quick to catch a mood or character. Unhappily, this natural talent withered when she wrote for publication in what she considered a "literary" style, painfully correct and stilted, full of careful allusions, lifeless. This affected even her writing for children. Already E. Nesbit's *The Treasure Seekers* had set a new standard of unsentimental realism in children's literature, while in 1902 Beatrix Potter's animals began to speak with their customary majestic authority. Yet in the *Enfield Observer*, Florence continued to write, as she was taught, of queenly lilies, furry bunnies and dainty dolls. A high moral tone seemed to be required by the readers. A New Year began, "How glorious it is to think that we can make the year a chaplet of golden days, each day bright with love and kindliness and unselfishness."[10] By far the most attractive of her articles are the descriptions of nature, which show spontaneous interest and pleasure in mottled plovers' eggs, glow-worms or frogs.

In summer 1903, while at home on sick-leave, and so free from the burden of teaching, Florence published her first article for adults over the initials F.E.D. "A Summer Lane"[11] is a rhapsodic account of wild flowers, "each one divine, a miracle of form and hue ... What does this beauty mean? What is its message?" She feels a deep pang of bitterness at leaving the lane for the hated town. "O Spirit of the green fields and hedgerows, genius of the summer lane, enter into me, and let thy life be mine!" The source of this style is not hard to trace, for Hyatt, a Richard Jefferies enthusiast, had recently brought out a book celebrating "all that is beautiful in nature". From his invalid's room, he traced the months of the year in an imaginary garden, a plan Florence was later to use in her book *In Lucy's Garden*. Hyatt took a conventional view of the countryside, with "cottagers busy in their little gardens", where "birds sing in pure thankfulness" and wild arum plants are "like to exquisitely carved cups of jade". The origin of Florence's country walk is here. "Nothing is more delightful than a stroll through our Middlesex lanes. What scene could be more fair?"[12] There is something deeply sad about the hunger for life and beauty which struggles through the stale language. Florence, taught from childhood to obey her teachers, modelled herself on this feverish style, so that readers commented on her "purple patches".[13]

Happily, this was not the whole extent of Hyatt's influence. He had a plantsman's knowledge of flowers, and taught Florence a love of gardening, which brought her many hours of pleasure all through her life. Moreover, although a stilted writer, Hyatt was an excellent anthologist, who became a successful editor of selections for the gift book market, bringing out three or four volumes every year. He was a ticket-holder and, whenever well enough, a regular reader at the British Museum, where he showed himself a true book-lover with an individual taste.[14] His selections guided Florence through the standard authors most admired in their day: Thackeray, Dickens, George Eliot, Emerson and Thoreau. Old gardens remained his first love; his unhackneyed choices included passages from Gerard's *Herbal*, the apothecary gardener John Parkinson, and Richard Burton's translation of the *Gulistan* or *Rose Garden*, by the twelfth-century poet Sa'adi of Isfahan. Hyatt's countryside anthologies, *The Footpath Way* and *The Winds of Heaven*, introduced Florence to a range of writers she would hardly have met without him: Crabbe, William Barnes, Thomas Love Peacock, George Darley, Henry Vaughan, Thomas Carew, Abraham Cowley and Thomas Tusser. Hardy was later surprised by the range of Florence's reading, and described her as a fine critic.[15] She owed her knowledge of books to the sick and struggling young writer of Enfield.

Hyatt also taught Florence the journalist's craft. By sharing his weekly column in the *Enfield Observer*, she learnt to prepare copy, to correct proofs, to check references or look up facts in a library. Because of this local experience, she could later offer herself as a freelance writer or amanuensis to writers, including, of course, Hardy. Moreover, although he could not enjoy ordinary social life, Hyatt was said to be in correspondence with "many well-known men of letters and publishers". He gave Florence introductions and encouraged her first attempts at book publication, when she adapted children's stories for a series of supplementary class-readers used in elementary schools.[16] Her first original story demanded a sacrifice of principle; overcoming her objections to organized religion,

Florence composed tracts for the Christian Knowledge Society. Some of the titles survive; *Tim's Sister*, *Jack Been's Reward*, *Little-lie-Abed* and *Jenny who did not like Christmas*. *Tim's Sister* is a typical Sunday School prize. Tim, an orphan boy, is wrongly accused of theft at the grocer's shop where he works. His sister Emmie has attempted to shield him from evil companions who bet on football matches, and finally clears him by her devotion. Other characters include an egregiously fatherly vicar and Emmie's employer, a dainty invalid lady who illuminates texts. In the last chapter brother and sister are confirmed together. Not surprisingly, the book lacks conviction, apart from the passages where Emmie, eschewing cheap finery and frizzled fringe, becomes "refined", as well as religious; these expressed Florence's own aspirations. In 1907 she wrote some longer stories of about a hundred pages each in Collins's *Tales for the Children* series of school readers, Nos. 10 and 20, *Old Time Tales* and *Country Life*. *Country Life*, which survives, perhaps gives a fair impression of these readers. It drew on Florence's children's column articles, and was designed to study nature through personified animals, Mr. and Mrs. Bunny Rabbit, Mr. Prickleback, Flurry the Fieldmouse and a character optimistically named Friendly Fox. The style is arch, but the tales show genuine sympathy with small animals. The most convincing show personal observation, of Bill Sykes, the bulldog who shared his kennel with a cat, or the tired, thirsty nanny goat, forced to draw a child's goat chaise. Most important for Florence, with Hyatt's help she had become, however humbly, a published writer.

There seems no doubt about the depth of the relationship with this first author, which lasted all through Florence's twenties. Hyatt gave her confidence and practical help; he was, she said, "the only person who ever loved me, for I am not loveable". She felt him "a friend who was more to me than anything else in the world, for whom I would *gladly* have died".[17] Yet both must have known there was no hope for the future; he would never be able to marry her or release her from teaching. While still a young woman Florence settled into a quiet melancholy, which later experience did little to dispel. "Life is altogether so sad—so infinitely sad," she wrote to one friend. She was to achieve many of her ambitions, yet the sense of loss persisted. "How sad life seems at times," she wrote, when she was Hardy's wife and mistress of Max Gate. "Indeed it is *always* sad, only sometimes we do not perceive the sadness."[18]

In 1906 Hyatt added to his collection of anthologies *The Pocket Thomas Hardy*, which Florence later said was her first introduction to her future husband.[19] Hardy wrote her two formal notes on 10 August 1905 and 2 January 1906, so it is not clear whether this remark implied a literary or a personal introduction.[20] At all events,

Hardy agreed to the anthology and wrote to his publisher, "we may as well let Mr. Hyatt publish the little book of extracts from my work, as he wishes," requesting only that they should be taken from the latest edition.[21]

During the summer of 1906, Hyatt completed and brought out his selections. *The Pocket Thomas Hardy* was a blue volume, four inches by six, which would genuinely slip into a pocket. It still forms a good introduction to Hardy's work. The poetry included wistful love poems which appealed to Florence: "In a Eweleaze near Weatherbury", possibly associated with Hardy's cousin, Tryphena Sparks, and "A Broken Appointment", inspired by his love for Mrs. Henniker. There was a puzzling hate poem, "The Ivy Wife", which, Florence later learnt, secretly described the writer's estranged wife. The prose included skilfully-chosen highlights from the Wessex novels: Gabriel Oak under the stars at Norcombe Hill, Tess toiling at the threshing machine, Jude searching through the mist for the distant spires and domes of Christminster, the brooding solitude of Egdon Heath firing to scarlet in autumn. For Florence, with her hunger for natural beauty, these passages held a mystical significance. Hardy's sense of "the disappointments which inflict a wound whose mark we carry to our graves" expressed her own inmost regrets. Her favourite passage was, in fact, newly written, the introduction to the 1895 edition of *A Pair of Blue Eyes*, with its description of the Cornish cliffs, "the ghostly birds, the pall like sea, the frothy wind, the eternal soliloquy of the waters". By an irony which Florence could not yet know, this was the country of Hardy's wife Emma, and their first romantic meeting. Perhaps what appealed to Florence most of all was the promise in the same novel that "anybody's life may be just as romantic or strange and interesting, if he or she fail or if he or she succeed". From the depths of a commonplace life, which seemed to offer so little hope of change in the future, she gratefully accepted the comfort of this assurance.[22]

The years were passing; the strands of Florence's life were beginning to come together and a future pattern to emerge. On 1 December 1906, she was granted a ticket of admission to the British Museum Reading Room; unfortunately the application form containing the name of her sponsor is not at present available to researchers.[23] In the same month, she took for the first time a holiday job away from home, which greatly widened her social horizons. In April 1907 Hardy rented a flat in Hyde Park Mansions for the London season, and spent considerable time in the Reading Room, where Florence volunteered to help with the checking and revising of Part III of *The Dynasts*. By the summer of 1907, the great writer and the young teacher were meeting regularly.

4

"A Scribbling Woman"

FLORENCE DUGDALE, in long skirt and frilled muslin blouse, was at twenty-eight a beautiful young woman. Hardy was sixty-seven, a small, grey, tired man, embittered by long estrangement from his once-loved wife and exhausted by the struggle to finish his epic drama of the Napoleonic wars, *The Dynasts*. He had started in high spirits; on a private visit to Madame Tussaud's waxworks, he had even tried on Wellington's cocked hat.[1] Now he felt he might die before finishing it. Yet if Florence had youth and beauty, Hardy had the compelling authority of England's greatest living writer. Florence was given to romantic dreams, yet how could she have dreamt a man of genius would take an interest in her? By 28 June 1907, he had inscribed and given her a copy of his *Wessex Poems*. Since, though of different generations, they were both Victorians, their talk soon turned to religion, where they discovered their shared unbelief. On 3 July came a copy of *The Rubaiyat of Omar Khayyam*, to seal this new bond between them; in all they gave each other twenty-four inscribed pocket volumes, which were sold after Florence's death.

Florence was awe-struck by the sight of Hardy revising *The Dynasts*; it was her first encounter with a great author and she felt "his mind was luminous".[2] It was a privilege to help him check the draft of Part III and look up references in the Reading Room. Nor, she later insisted, was she paid for this work, though two surviving letters from Hardy to her during 1907 in fact deal with it.[3] Hardy escorted his young amanuensis to Liverpool Street Station and watched her slender form vanish towards the Enfield train, a scene movingly re-created in *On the Departure Platform*.

> A wee white spot of muslin fluff
> That down the diminishing platform bore
> Through hustling crowds of gentle and rough
>   To the carriage door.

> Under the lamplight's fitful glowers
> Behind dark groups from far and near,
> Whose interests were apart from ours,
>   She would disappear,

30

3   Florence Dugdale in her twenties

Then show again, till I ceased to see
That flexible form, that nebulous white;
And she who was more than my life to me
    Had vanished quite ...

After years of *The Idylls of the King*, how did it feel to find this
vein of poetry in everyday life, still more to find her everyday self
at the heart of it? As though in self-defence, Florence insisted that
Hardy's obvious emotion was "quite apart from passion", rather
"a tender, protective affection for me, as a father for a child".[4] Nor,
to her credit, did she pretend to be in love with this man older than
her own father. Florence, emancipated from religion, remained a
true Victorian where sex was concerned. She disliked the "mania
about sex" in May Sinclair's harmless novels, and "the suspicion
of something rather unpleasant" in E. F. Benson. When Marie
Stopes sent her a book, she was embarrassed and apologetic; "pray
forgive me, I don't much appreciate the love-making, a lack of real
feeling on my part, I suppose."[5] She even complained, when married
to the creator of Tess, "how disgustingly country people of the servant class talk".[6]

Hardy inspired this young teacher with feelings of awe, amaze-
ment and the extreme deference she had been taught to show to
authority. Moreover, she had thwarted ambitions as a writer, which
children's readers could never satisfy; she mentioned at different
times short stories, a play and a psychological novel. Hardy, usually
so scornful of journalists, offered endless help and encouragement
to the aspirant from the *Enfield Observer*. He wrote a letter to his
own publisher, Frederick Macmillan, and next day a similar letter
to Archibald Marshall, literary editor of the *Daily Mail*. He spoke of
Florence's strong literary tastes and natural gift for writing, her experience of children, her "old Dorset family" and his conviction that
she was "capable of doing more important work than the drudgery
of teaching" ... "I shall be greatly obliged if you will see her."[7] Few
editors in London would be likely to refuse Hardy's personal request.
Florence had visiting cards printed with the address River Front,
leaving out the number, which revealed this was one of a street of
houses.[8] With more experience of the world, Florence might have
guessed the curiosity Hardy's letters would arouse. Both men
interviewed her, during the summer holidays of 1907, but neither
offered her employment and she was reluctantly forced to return
to teaching in the autumn.

The next step, apparently trivial, formed a turning point for
Florence's character, more serious perhaps than she could allow herself to realize. In September 1907, Hardy sent to the *Cornhill Magazine* a short story signed F. E. Dugdale. The editor replied with a
certain sly humour: "I am writing to Miss (I take it the author is
a lady?) Dugdale to accept the story for the *Cornhill Magazine*. Only
I wish I could print with it your words of praise? Then it would
surely be read."[9] On these somewhat ambiguous terms, Florence
seemed at last to have achieved her life's ambition. She was accepted
for publication in a distinguished London periodical, in the company of G. M. Trevelyan, A. W. Pollard and the future Virginia
Woolf. At twenty-eight, as if by magic, she was a literary woman.
A closer look at the story itself shows at what cost to personal integ-
rity this had been achieved.

The Apotheosis of the Minx, subtitled "A Study from the Life of
the Many", is a curious product. The setting and the opening pages
are clearly created by Florence from her own experience: a class of
restless boys, a dreary school in an asphalt playground, a depressing
street of "smoky dwarf houses". Robert Engle, the young elementary school teacher, "pale of cheek and narrow-chested", with "a
love of poetry over-keen", and his worship of "the beauty of earth
and sky", owed something to the invalid Alfred Hyatt and more perhaps to Florence herself. His work "held him captive as a maimed
rabbit in a steel trap"; this was by now certainly Florence's view of

her life as a teacher. Yet the story develops in a way strangely typical of Hardy. The poetry-lover falls in love with a vulgar, greedy dress-maker's assistant. This ill-assorted pair go for a walk in the country, which might have come straight from the opening of Hardy's *Jude the Obscure*. Robert, sexually innocent, expects Etty to enjoy a country ramble, but she is bored and irritated. "To her mind, Robert Engle had no 'go' in him." Beside, she has met a shop assistant with splendid black moustaches, a sort of Alec d'Urberville of the grocery counter. She taunts Robert and leaves him full of bitterness; when she marries the grocer, he forgets her "cheap fascinations". Etty dies, and on a Sunday walk past "the gate of the nearest ceme-tery"—a Hardyesque touch—Engle meets her black-clad widower. He learns that he was the one she had really loved. "'It was your intellect I suppose,' said the grocer sadly. 'She used to say you were such a refined man.'" Later he meets the grocer again, jaunty, spruce and about to re-marry. Now the schoolmaster is free to ideal-ize his dead dressmaker. This commonplace girl, once dead, becomes an object of worship; "happy, beautiful, pure and spiritual beyond earthly women, she was now *His*."[10] This irony was completely characteristic of Hardy. Indeed, as Florence was to learn, he would one day re-enact it in his own life, and hers. Her slight and sentimen-tal story had been revised and completely transformed by his master hand. Without this it seems doubtful that the *Cornhill* would have published F. E. Dugdale's contribution, for her talent was small. Like her hero Robert, "every poetic instinct was there, but it seemed as if expression had been denied". Instead, she was more than once party to a literary deception.

Until now there had been little to distinguish Florence from hundreds of girls of her background and time, with the same training and the same aspirations; but meeting Hardy had inescapably changed her life. From now on she would be an ordinary person in an extraordinary situation, sharply exposed to public curiosity. In December 1907 she fell ill again; a cold turned to influenza and she was unable to teach for three weeks. Former pupils recall tension between her and her father, though at this distance in time no one could be sure. Hardy dreaded that harm might come to her "delicate throat"; she was, he wrote, altogether so "fearfully delicate".[11] In February 1908 she at last went to see a London throat specialist, who advised rest and a change for her general debility. The Enfield Education Committee gave her three months' leave of absence, which began on 8 April.[12] Florence appears never to have returned to teaching, even for a day.

In May 1908 Hardy was installed in a tiny back-room at a hotel in Southampton Row, convenient for the British Museum; he wrote urging his wife against "venturing up here"[13] in the abnormally hot summer. Editors habitually pursued him with requests for contributions, none more indefatigably than Clement Shorter, of the middle-brow pictorial weekly, *The Sphere*. Hardy did not greatly care for Shorter or his wife, the Irish nationalist poet Dora Sigerson. Yet in May 1908, Shorter was planning a full-page *Sphere* feature on the new loop line of the Great Northern Railway from Enfield to Hertford, which appeared at the end of the month. The technical parts of this article were clearly written by a railway engineer, but the local colour, both in style and content, suggests Florence's hand. The great houses, parks and gardens of the district are described in the style of a local guidebook, which Alfred Hyatt was writing at exactly this time.[14] Florence, who always explained that she lived in "the more countrified and prettier part of Enfield", may well have written the descriptions, which stress rural gentility. The new trains would pass through a country of "picturesque charms and breezy, health-giving uplands ... beautifully wooded and undulating". Any development would be select, "a high-class residential area ... the jerry-builder will be warned off the route".[15] A fortnight before the Enfield railway article was published, Mr. Dugdale had reported his daughter's resignation on medical grounds to the Enfield Education Committee; "Miss F. Dugdale was unable to continue owing to her chronic pharyngitis returning."[16] A reasonable inference is that Hardy had once again appealed to an editor on Florence's behalf, as he had done the previous summer, but this time successfully, and that along with her old pharyngitis Miss Dugdale had a new job.

There is scattered evidence of Florence's career as a journalist, which started in June 1908. She set off hopefully for the *Sphere* offices, in Great New Street, Fetter Lane, between Dr. Johnson's house in Gough Square and Dickens's rooms in Furnivall's Inn, at the heart of literary London. She saw in herself "the journalistic spirit"; she would be "a scribbling woman". Reality, after these romantic dreams, proved a shattering disappointment. Even before her weeks of preliminary training were over, she tried to resign; she felt that she hated the work and the drab, dirty London streets, so unlike anything she had imagined. In this crisis, Clement Shorter talked to her "very kindly and very sensibly", as she afterwards felt.[17] He sympathized with Florence's efforts to educate herself and become a writer, for he too had earned his own living from the age of fourteen and picked up knowledge by reading at second-hand bookstalls, until he was equipped to enter "pictorial journalism". He pointed out that he had done his best to give Florence what she wanted, "work that other literary women would have jumped to get". It was not fair to him or the paper to throw it up after a month or two, just when she was becoming useful.[18] Florence responded to this appeal and carried on for six months, although by now she regretted the whole venture. She said that Shorter "had been very kind, giving me literary work, reviewing etc.";[19] this was a later embellishment of her original employment on the paper.

The Sphere was an illustrated weekly "for the home". Apart from Shorter's own "Literary Letter" and brief columns on politics, sport and the theatre, the text consisted of captions to pictures of royalty, the Empire, the armed forces, society recreations and spectacular disasters. These faithfully reflected the interests of its middle-class readers. There was also a feature called "About women's sphere and influence", which embraced cookery, children, the doings of society hostesses, and while Florence was on the staff, the wedding of Mr. and Mrs. Winston Churchill, at which the happy couple received ten cigarette boxes and twenty-one inkstands.[20] Florence later boasted mildly to Hardy's American admirer, Miss Owen, that "I went to a reception once at the American Embassy in Park Lane when the Whitelaw Reids were there. How well I remember the magnificence. And her *pearls*!"[21] This innocent name-dropping suggests that Florence was "Angela", fashion correspondent to *The Sphere*, who in the last week of June 1908 attended the wedding reception for the Ambassador's daughter Miss Jean Reid and the Hon. John Ward. The dresses are described and the bride photographed wearing an apparently suffocating pearl choker.[22] Over the years Florence had remembered the glittering occasion, but her romantic imagination had transformed the circumstances in which she took part.

The job, though not the literary career Florence had dreamt of, was by no means completely dull; "Angela" became a mouthpiece during the next few months for some of her genuine interests. Disused farmhouses should become children's homes with gardens attached, "and thus a love of nature inculcated".[23] "Making the life of little children happier", a need Florence knew from her ten years of elementary teaching, appeared under various headings: children's charities, country outings, free school dinners for the needy. Animals always received sympathetic coverage, including a vast tabby cat which presided over the women's prison at Aylesbury—"the prisoners adore this animal"—and a wire-haired terrier which saved its master's life by barking when a fire broke out.[24] As visitors to Max Gate would later learn to their cost, this was always Florence's favourite breed. The women's movement, or "Symptoms of Suffragitis", by contrast, aroused "Angela's" hostility.[25] This seems to have been because it concerned politics, for the social plight of the "poor gentlewoman" or "educated poor lady", as Florence saw herself, was a recurrent theme. These women, who could not afford Harley Street, needed "lady doctors in district surgeries", something which Florence, with her persistent ill-health, knew from personal experience. Another need for ladies who had to earn their livings, was "more work that pertains altogether to women's world".[26] Two of the careers "Angela" recommended, nursing and domestic science teaching, were in fact followed by Florence's youngest sisters. Another, landscape gardening, was an interest she shared with Alfred Hyatt. Florence, now almost thirty, was still devoted to her "poor young writer friend", whom she recommended to the Shorters. Hyatt included a poem by Shorter's wife, Dora Sigerson, in *The Winds of Heaven* and Shorter gave the new anthology a kindly notice in his Literary Letter of 2 January 1909.

In literary style, Florence was still Hyatt's pupil, sometimes with bizarre effect. Her account of a new perfume "into which is incorporated all the fragrant, delicate and mysterious sweetness of an Eastern garden",[27] reads like a straight crib from his version of Sa'adi's *Rose Garden*. The literary models she had long studied so conscientiously were now adapted to the breathless urgency of the fashion-writer's craft. "Angela" dealt with "the new semi-divided skirt", the "crusader motor casque" and the "fragile blouses" to which, by his own account, Thomas Hardy was so susceptible. Florence gave fashion its due, even when it put a strain on grammar; a lady's "pretty gown of white crêpe de chine elaborated with silver embroidery and Irish lace on the decolletage and a train of white brocade was much admired". Nor did she later lose her eye for dress, when as Hardy's wife she came to move in distinguished circles. Lady Londonderry "had lovely large diamond and pearl earrings and wore a black hat that suited her. She left in the hall a lovely brown motoring coat, lined with wool."[28] The ideal lady of fashion was Hardy's charming former flame, the Hon. Mrs. Henniker, "who looked handsomer than I have ever before seen her. She was dressed exquisitely ... in cream lace with touches of turquoise and green and a lovely hat of green with turquoise."[29] There is a professional authority in these pronouncements.

Florence's brief foray into journalism suggests that she shared all the normal interests of middle-class women of her times. It is sad and puzzling that she came to feel, "the thing I am really sorry I did was to attempt newspaper work, for I found after six months of it that it was the most degrading work anybody could take up— typewriting is a lady's occupation by comparison."[30] She hated commuting to work through the horrifying slums north of Liverpool Street station. Characteristically, her mind did not turn to political or public remedies, but to the ugliness; "awful pictures of North London and the horrible Dalston there ... the train journey alas is a horrid one".[31] The summer of 1908 was particularly hot and sultry, the winter months bitterly cold with snow and ice. There may have been jealousy in *The Sphere's* office, where Florence, a complete novice, had secured a coveted job through Hardy's patronage. As "Angela" primly put it, "jealousy of each other in their work is women's great weakness". Florence wrote more bluntly, "women are the meanest of created things";[32] it is not hard to see why she got on better with men. Did she overhear some of the gossip and speculation which must have surrounded her at work? Hardy recoiled from journalistic gossip, but his indiscriminate praise of Florence's talents—"she writes original things, is a splendid proof reader and a fine critic, her taste in poetry being unerring"[33]—must have raised some eyebrows in cynical Fleet Street.

Moreover journalism on a picture paper proved to have the same lowly social status as elementary teaching. She went, as a *Sphere* picture shows, in evening dress to balls and society receptions, but once there, her standing was little higher than that of a typist. It is not hard to imagine the casual insults to which a pretty working girl might be exposed in Edwardian London, or how they offended Florence's view of herself as an educated gentlewoman. By contrast, "writing children's stories was quite harmless", and she could place them in juvenile magazines or annuals. Early in 1909 she resigned. Meanwhile, though, there was one great house where she would be accepted on an equal footing, and "dear, kind friends" who would offer her shelter.

5

"Dear, Kind Friends"

THE MOST mysterious of Florence Dugdale's occasional remarks about her early life refer to "my dear, kind friends in
Dublin",[1] or to a great "house in Dublin where I used to stay before
the husband and wife both died". These friends were evidently
devoted to her, and gave her a typewriter "to help me with my
literary work in which they took so great an interest".[2] In return,
she wrote regularly every week to "my dear, lost friends", making
sure that the letters should always reach them by Sunday morning.
As for the Dublin house, it was "more luxurious" than Lady Jeune's
in Portland Place, Lady Hoare's Stourhead, or even Melbury, with
its lion gates and prospect tower.[3] How did a young teacher from
outer London come to form this unlikely, but close relationship?

The answer, as so often, lies in Florence herself, the clinging,
romancing strain in her nature, which entwined itself round ordinary
working relationships, and often evoked a response from others. The
relationship in this case was that of invalid's companion. The idea
of being a companion suggested itself naturally to Florence, since
her mother, although she was to live until 1929, frequently required
home nursing, which the sisters shared. Mrs. Dugdale had a serious
skin condition and the dermatologist from Eva's training hospital
at Tottenham warned the family that they must be "very, very careful" of her. Also, when suffering from depression, Mrs. Dugdale could
not be left alone. Florence wrote that she cooked invalid dishes for
her mother, ran up and down stairs with trays, dressed and ban-
daged her legs, went for cautious outings in good weather, or read
aloud when it rained. She was gentle, patient and "loved taking care
of people".[4] This experience fitted Florence for the numerous resident posts, advertised each week on the back page of *The Times*,
at a salary of forty to fifty pounds, a year, for "refined" or
"cultured" ladies' companions. In addition, as "Angela" in *The
Sphere*, Florence cautioned her readers against fraudulent agencies
which "extract fees from poor gentlewomen" seeking such posts.[5]

Why was Florence prepared to consider a life of dependency, such
as her mother, a Victorian governess, had known? At first sight it
seems an unenterprising choice for a young woman of the twentieth
century. Already Jane Harrison had published her *Prolegomena to
the Study of Greek Religion*, while Constance Garnett had introduced

the British reading public to Turgenev and Gogol, Tolstoi and Dos-
toievski. Women physicians, social workers and factory inspectors
were accepted in their professions, while women administrators in
school or hospital received a respect tinged with awe. Yet Florence
Dugdale's situation was typical of many women without capital or
professional family background. She explicitly accepted the dependence of women upon men as right and proper, like her untrained
contemporaries who formed the army of impoverished widows after
the Great War.

Florence first took a post as temporary companion during the
winter of 1906–7, fifteen months before she finally gave up teaching.
This first post came in the same month that she received her British
Museum reader's ticket, and fairly shortly after her early meetings
with Hardy. The details remain obscure, but she was possibly recommended by Mrs. Clement Shorter, whose father was a well-known
Dublin physician. Dr. Sigerson of Merrion Square "knew every one
in Dublin",[6] including his neighbour, the famous surgeon Sir Thornley Stoker, who needed an assistant companion for his invalid wife.
Florence may have acted as holiday relief for the regular companion
during her own school holidays, since her mother wrote to her, care
of Lady Stoker, for the new year of 1907.[7] Later, having left both
teaching and journalism, she stayed for longer periods, although she
was studiously vague about the details of her employment. Neither
in this, nor later similar posts, did she ever write of a post or salary.
She was simply "staying with friends" and she soon established herself on terms of genuine affection with a series of employers.[8]

The post with Sir Thornley and Lady Stoker formed a turning
point in Florence's life, second only to her meeting with Hardy.
Naturally adept at the protective camouflage of the lady companion,
she entered into a way of life which she had never known. No experience in later life could blot from her memory the first sight of Ely
House, perhaps the most perfect Georgian mansion in Dublin. Its
full breadth of nine windows faced the sober elegance of Ely Place.
The visitor was admitted by Sir Thornley's butler; "such a boon
and a blessing to have a good manservant in the house", wrote
Florence wistfully in leaner days.[9] On the ground floor lay dining
and consulting rooms with magnificent Adam stucco work; a Far-
nese Hercules stood poised at the foot of the grand stair. Above were
two lovely, light drawing-rooms with marble chimneypieces and
silver grates, and on the top floor eight spacious bedrooms.[10] At sun-
down the great gates of Ely Place were closed; neither carriages nor
walkers disturbed the quiet greensward and the trees.

The Stokers had worked with loving care to restore this palace
to the style in which it had been built in 1736, by an extravagant
Marquess of Ely. They appeared to be living, by the light of wax

candles and Waterford glass chandeliers, in the eighteenth century.
They had been married since before Florence was born, and kept
open house with cheerful generosity to artists, writers, politicians
and scientists. Guests, even strangers, felt at home in the magic circle
of Emily Stoker's intelligence, kindness and charm. When she fell
ill, friends and neighbours, including George Moore, flocked to the
house to make enquiries, but were told only that "her malady was
likely to be long and painful".[11] In fact she was slowly losing her
reason, but Sir Thornley Stoker was determined to protect his wife
from the stigma of insanity, then very real. A trustworthy nurse,
Betty Webb, came, officially as a secretary, but really to take care
of her; Florence, as secretary-receptionist, became Miss Webb's
assistant, a confidential post which she filled with great conscientiousness.[12] She answered letters, read aloud, and exercised the
yapping black Pomeranian, which had the distinction of having
bitten George Moore. There was no menial work to be done, for the
great house had a lavish staff of Irish servants and Florence was
free to devote herself to "my dear, dear, friend Lady Stoker",[13] of
whom she was genuinely fond. The Stokers were a tragic couple,
lonely, childless, their beautiful house overshadowed by illness
which could only grow worse. A young face was welcome, and events
were to prove that they grew very fond of Florence in return.

Sir Thornley Stoker was famous for his kind heart; students,
young doctors, the nurses at the Richmond Hospital, poor patients
in the workhouse wards, even the laboratory animals, found a friend
in him. The great hall at the Royal College of Surgeons was not large
enough to hold all the friends who wanted to give him a dinner on
the occasion of his knighthood. At sixty-four he was near the end
of his brilliant career as a surgeon and teacher of surgery, but he
still took what an Irish writer called "a warm and *fighting* interest
in Poor Law and Hospital reform".[14] Cruelty made him angry;
otherwise he was charming, amusing, immensely popular, and only
close friends knew the cares of what Gogarty called "his kind but
troubled heart".[15] From this employer, Florence acquired an education in the arts. He was interested in painting, music, the theatre,
through his brother Bram, who was Irving's manager. Above all,
Stoker was a connoisseur. Moore, a caustic neighbour, liked to make
fun of the famous surgeon's collection. "The Chinese Chippendale
mirror over the drawing-room chimneypiece originated in an un-
successful operation for cancer; the Aubusson carpet in the back
drawing room represents a hernia; the Renaissance bronze on the
landing a set of gall-stones; the Ming cloisonée a floating kidney;
the Buhl cabinet his opinion on a liver; and Lady Stoker's jewels
a series of small operations over a number of years."[16] But to
Florence, hungry for beauty and distinction, Ely House was a fairy

4 Sir Thornley Stoker

palace. Sir Thornley loved to show and talk about his treasures, stroking the "skin" of a fine mahogany piece with clinical care. He showed the admiring Florence Chippendale, Adam, Queen Anne and Louis XVI furniture, old Irish silver, Waterford glass, Chinese export porcelain, Japanese lacquer work, fifteenth-century Italian bronzes, French clocks, Persian rugs, first editions in fine bindings, miniatures and antique jewelry: all the spoils of forty years' collecting.[17] Florence, a diligent student, learnt it all; this seems to have been the origin of her careful good taste, so derided by Somerset Maugham in the person of Mrs. Driffield.

At Ely House, Florence learnt a way of life she had read of, but can hardly have experienced before. With instinctive compliance, she adapted herself to the Stokers' outlook, tastes and manners. If her bizarre account of the second General Election of 1910 is anything to go by, she even took on their Unionist politics in which the Liberal party's appeal to the Irish vote was part of a sinister conspiracy. "Roman Catholic priests all over the country have given orders to their followers to vote Liberal—for the aim of this election is to get Home Rule for Ireland, so that the R.C. religion may be firmly established there and then they can work from there. Mr. Asquith is fully aware of this, but he is in league with the R.C.s."[18] Much in this new society was puzzling. There was for instance George Moore at No. 4 Ely Place, working every day with his long-suffering secretary Miss Parrish.[19] "The things he writes about are disgusting and he is a horrible man," wrote Florence later, "but sometimes he writes the most exquisite, the most peerless English." Miss Parrish was even more of a puzzle, since she later published a novel, in which Florence believed she must have been "aided by George Moore".[20] Apart from the inherent improbability of Moore helping another writer, since G. T. Parrish later wrote the haunting and individual *Madame Solario*, this could hardly have been more mistaken. Yet it is striking that Florence believed a successful woman writer *must* have been helped by a man. Could she possibly have been persuaded that this was a normal way to work? Another Ely Place neighbour, young Dr. St. John Gogarty, was also a puzzle. Sir Thornley kindly sent him patients, and he entertained the whole neighbourhood with lampoons, limericks and anecdotes—but how much of what he said was true? Strangely, no one seemed to care.[21] This cultured and exclusive society fixed the level of Florence's social aspirations for life.

It is not known if Florence told the Stokers about her early struggles to educate herself and become a writer, something which even in Edwardian society must have won sympathy and respect. She certainly seems to have talked freely about a subject near her heart, the hardships of the "educated, poor lady", whom she considered "in many ways worse off than the poorest of the poor with free schools and improved workhouses". She told them of the children's stories which she wrote, but that "the cost of having my MSS typewritten for me ran away with much of the scanty payment I got". Sir Thornley, whose generosity was a byword, promptly bought her a typewriter. Florence was delighted, but, morbidly sensitive in matters of social standing, later pointed out that she was "not a typist".[22] She talked of her sister who was a nurse; indeed she had a photograph taken in 1910 of Eva, in Sister Dora cap, with bow under the chin. Sir Thornley, who had introduced nurse-training at his own hospital, took a kindly interest and recommended

Eva for a nursing post with his brother Bram's friends, the Irvings. Florence's artless account of this shows exactly the blend of wistful fantasy and wish-fulfilment with which she regarded such posts. "The Laurence Irvings were friends of a great friend of mine . . . my sister looked after her a great deal and fell desperately in love with them and used to write me glowing letters and tell me what they had promised to do when they came back from America. She was going to stay with them and so forth."[23] These high hopes came tragically to nothing, for the Irvings on their homeward journey were drowned in a shipwreck. There must have been many such dreams doomed to disappointment in the lives of women who lived as dependants in upper-class households.

There is no evidence that Florence was at home in Enfield or in London for much of 1909 and 1910; although the dates are unknown it seems possible that the Stokers needed her for longer periods. Sir Thornley was made a baronet in the accession honours of King George V, which gave pleasure to his host of friends. To him it must have been a hollow distinction, for he had no heir and his wife was deteriorating fast. "Sir Thornley", said a sympathetic colleague at the Richmond Hospital, "has hell at home."[24] Miss Webb was excellent and reliable, Florence patient and devoted, but it must have been increasingly hard to keep up a semblance of normality in this once-proud household. During the salmon-fishing season Sir Thornley liked to take a rod on the Slaney, and one evening invited a bachelor party, including George Moore, Augustine Birrell and Gogarty, to sample his catch. The guests were gathered round the candle-lit table and the host was chining the salmon, when, wrote Gogarty: "At this stage the mahogany door burst open, and a nude and elderly lady came in with a cry, 'I like a little intelligent conversation!' She ran round the table. We all stood up. She was followed by two female attendants, who seized whatever napery was available, and sheltering her with this and their own bodies, led her forth screaming from the room. All this time Sir Thornley, with his knuckles on the table, inclined his head as though saying a silent grace."[25] Gogarty's anecdotes were usually embroidered, but this one was well attested. The names of the two attendants in this macabre scene were, of course, not given, but the two recorded in Sir Thornley's will, apparently as companions to his wife, were Betty Webb and Florence Dugdale.

The case was now tragically beyond home care. Lady Stoker was moved, perhaps to the nursing-home where she died in November 1910. Sir Thornley had already in July put the lease of Ely House up for sale and in June Florence was at home and available for work in London.[26] If she had seen this sad conclusion at first hand, it is hardly surprising she later came to believe that the aggrieved,

5   Florence Dugdale aged about 30

irascible Emma Hardy had been "a mad wife" and that human existence was essentially a tragic affair. Nor was this the only relic of Florence's time in Dublin, for her pliant, submissive nature changed fast in strange surroundings. She gained wider experience of life, with apparent sophistication and social standing. Yet these were bought at a price, for she lost her independence. No longer did she struggle to make a career against the odds and on her own. From now on she came to live increasingly in the lives of older people with an assured status, seeing the world through their eyes and looking with them towards the past. "I feel a hateful little snob," she later confessed, but she continued to find the gentry "easier and nicer" than her equals.[27] For a young woman, this was sometimes to be a very lonely existence. There remained however one clear gain. In later years, even those who smiled at poor Florence's intellectual and social pretensions[28] found her care of the aged Hardy admirable. Many accounts agree on the quiet routine, the careful diet, the exclusion of annoying visitors, the low voice reading aloud, the endless patience, which fostered and protected Hardy's late work. It now seems that Florence may have learnt this exacting discipline with a difficult patient, an experienced nurse, and a great medical teacher during her spells of duty at Ely House.

6

"Times Not Easy"

AS PROOF of her new sophistication, Florence acquired a London club, when, by July 1909, she had joined the Lyceum at 128 Piccadilly. This described itself as "a meeting-place for women who are in touch with the best work of Art, Literature, Music and Public Service of every kind". Here Florence could attend Orchestral Teas to the strains of the Ladies' Amateur Orchestra, Poetry Circle Conversaziones, a Shakespeare Fancy Dress Dance, Novelists' Dinners with popular authors (Hardy had once been approached), Oriental lectures or monthly debates on topics like Total Abstinence or the Bird Plumage Bill.[1] Florence was innocently delighted to be a fellow-member with the best-selling novelists, "Rita" and Marie Corelli. She invited relatives and friends to tea at the Lyceum, explaining that, though her means were limited, it was essential to join a good club, "in order to meet people in the literary world". She introduced herself to the novelist May Sinclair, who was anxious for an introduction to Hardy and, later, for a visit to Max Gate, though this did not happen, because "poor Mrs. H. says she *won't* have her (M.S.) at Max Gate, so what is poor Mr. T. H. to do?"[2] Florence also introduced herself as Hardy's secretary to another woman novelist, Netta Syrett, who agreed to address an Enfield literary club, but afterwards complained of a "badly-lighted, dreary little hall and a very uninspiring audience". She also found Hardy, duly produced for afternoon tea in London, "very uninspiring to talk to".[3] It seems, though, that as Hardy's London secretary, Florence enjoyed a privileged position among the literary ladies at the Lyceum.

At home in Enfield, too, knowing Hardy had subtly changed her status. In the first week of December 1909, she gave a paper on him and his newly-published book of poems, *Time's Laughingstocks*, to the local literary society, which, according to the *Enfield Observer*, "proved most able and interesting." She spoke of Hardy's early desire to enter the Church, his "loftiest motives even if they were ill-judged" in writing *Jude the Obscure*, and his "perfection of workmanship. He reveals to the reader the true romance of country life". This verdict on the sufferings of Tess and Jude seems to have passed unchallenged in Enfield, where Florence now became the only member of her family to visit the Chairman of the Education Committee. Vernon Gibberd was a handsome widower with two children, and he appreciated the company of literary or intellectual women. Florence seems to have been very fond of his little boy, Alan, to whom she later dedicated her book, *In Lucy's Garden*; yet it was the elder sister Kathleen who observed her with a child's sharp perception. "Miss Dugdale was said to work for Thomas Hardy. Was she his secretary? ... I have a feeling she was in Enfield intermittently. As I try to recapture my child's awareness of her, she seemed tall (to me), dark and remote from trivialities like perfunctory talk. I don't think she took any notice of me, for she seemed preoccupied in sharing literary confidences with my father."[4] This account confirms Florence's cult of literature, and her sense of isolation in society, both noted by later observers.

Her own literary work between 1909 and 1911 is difficult to trace; she mentions Blackie's children's annuals and *The Girl's Own Paper*, and in 1909 published another animal tale, *The Story of Mr. Prickleback*, a Story Reader for the Oxford University Press, Hardy's most recent publisher. She later complained of the wretched pay, but by living at home she made ends meet. "Writing children's stories was quite harmless and for years I earned a living at it, being shamefully treated by a big publishing firm, so everybody tells me now."[5] It cannot have been easy, yet she was still determined to be in whatever sense a writer. Hardy continued to help her with introductions, which might further her work, and worried about her continuing ill-health.

On 5 July 1909, Hardy had a long talk with a friend of almost twenty years' standing, his fellow-rationalist Edward Clodd. Clodd was the same age as Hardy, the son of chapel-going parents in Aldeburgh who had hoped to make him a Baptist minister. Instead he became a self-made businessman and secretary to a bank. In his spare time Clodd wrote a number of Darwinian studies, which put him on Emma Hardy's personal black list of bad influences on her husband. Clodd, with a grown-up family, was separated from his own wife and sympathetic to Hardy's "strained relations"; he was also an essentially kindly man, proud of his literary friends and always ready to help them. This free-thinking, advanced but extremely respectable friend now heard about Hardy's "amanuensis",[6] who was later described as "my young friend and assistant ... I have known her for several years and am very anxious about her health and welfare and am determined to get her away to the seaside, or she will break down quite ... She is not really what is called a 'typist'," added Hardy carefully, "but as she learns anything, she has learnt that ... only doing my typewriting as a fancy."[7] Clodd took the hint and invited them both to his house at Aldeburgh, but the visit was put off twice because Florence was unwell.

Meanwhile she was at the centre of another crisis. Hardy wanted

6   Thomas Hardy at 69, painted by his sister Mary

to take her to the first night of the opera *Tess of the d'Urbervilles* by D'Erlanger at Covent Garden, but to his dismay Emma elected to come up from Dorset for the occasion. He therefore offered tickets to Clodd, who called for Florence at the Lyceum, meeting her for the first time, took her to dinner at the Gaiety Restaurant and escorted her to the Opera House. "If it should be a wet evening," Hardy had implored, "please make her wrap up as she is very delicate."[8] Florence enjoyed her evening, though they discreetly "left just before the end. I cabbed her to the Lyceum Club."[9] This kindly older man became for some years one of Florence's principal allies and confidants.

The postponed visit to Aldeburgh took place on 13 August. "She has been very unwell," explained Clodd tolerantly to Clement Shorter, "and Hardy told me he wants to give her a change, but 'times not easy' (Emma intervening?) so I suggested their coming to me at which he jumped."[10] Florence was inexperienced and shared with Hardy a curiously bookish attitude to real life situations; she seemed not to realize the arrangement might cause gossip. In the train going down to Suffolk she talked happily about the countryside, which was new to her. Clodd's house-parties at Strafford House, Aldeburgh, were an institution, and Hardy was a precious centrepiece in his gatherings. As a fellow-guest wrote,

> How late we tarried, slow and tardy,
> Yet loth to lose one tale from Hardy!

On this occasion, however, Clodd had tactfully invited Hardy and Florence alone. The sea air revived her, the two old gentlemen agreed, "wonderfully"; she delighted in the friendly house, the fishermen's boats, the golden gorse commons, the limitless skies of East Anglia, and the channel of the river Alde winding its way through salt marshes to the sea. Both felt convinced that Clodd was, as Florence later put it, "completely safe". On 16 August Hardy even agreed to be photographed with Florence on the shingle beach,[11] one of the happiest and most spontaneous likenesses of him ever taken. Clodd's diary dates this photograph for the first time.

The weather was beautiful and Florence loved sailing in Clodd's boat, the *Lotus*, so he proposed a water-picnic at Iken. Returning after lunch, through the treacherous tidal shallows of the Alde, they met "calamity unparalleled". The boatman attempted to take a short cut and landed them on a mud bank, where the tide would not lift them off for another twelve hours. They flew a flag of distress, Hardy "vigorously waved his pocket handkerchief" and a passing craft sent "a relief expedition to a small and anxious party". They landed at Aldeburgh Quay at nine that evening, Clodd "chaffing" Hardy, as he liked to do, about imaginary reports in the local paper:

7   Florence and Hardy on Aldeburgh beach, taken by an amateur photo-
grapher on 16 August 1909

"Perilous Position of England's Greatest Novelist: Rescue of the
Illustrious by Brave Boatmen of Aldeburgh."[12] Not even this alarming prospect clouded Hardy's serenity. He had announced that
Florence would work for him; there would be a "clicking of the type-
writer". In the event, Florence did not even complete the children's
story she was supposed to be writing. Instead, during their ten days'
visit, he took her out, to Cromer, where he sent a card to his sister
Kate, and to Norwich.[13] No trouble was too great to give Florence
pleasure. "Hardy and the Lady are enjoying themselves," wrote
Clodd to the ever-interested Shorter.[14] To these two admirers of
Meredith, "The Lady" represented the Other Woman in Meredith's
Modern Love, but Florence, returning rested and refreshed to
Enfield, seemed quite unaware of these overtones to her seaside
holiday.
     The Easter and autumn visits to Aldeburgh became an institution
with a pattern of their own, which lasted until the death of Emma

Hardy in 1912. At Easter 1910, Clodd tried the experiment of adding another couple, "Whymper et uxor". Perhaps this was an attempt to provide young company for Florence, for though the great alpinist was now seventy, his new wife, who later divorced him, was a girl of twenty-two. Hardy was in good form; he read his poem on Swinburne, whose grave in the Isle of Wight he had just visited with Florence. He also read his sonnet *Zermatt: to the Matterhorn*, describing "that day's tragic feat of manly might", inspired by Chapter 22 of Whymper's *Scrambles in the Alps*, describing how three of his fellow-climbers and their guide were killed on the mountain. Whymper traced in red ink on the map the route taken by the doomed party in 1865; this somewhat grim evening's entertainment was "at Mr. Hardy's desire".[15] At other times, more happily, he read them new poems, or there was literary talk with "amusing things to say" about Hardy's bête noire, the religious best-seller Hall Caine.[16] In 1911 and 1912 the Clement Shorters joined the house-party, and the two women went for a trial trip in Clodd's new boat. It was a whole new world of experience for Florence; she told Clodd with complete sincerity what a treat these sociable, hospitable holidays were in her often lonely life.[17] She also got to know Hardy better, though significantly she knew him only in holiday mood.[18]

On these visits to Aldeburgh, Clodd won Florence's confidence by his genuine kindness and concern for her welfare. She told him a good deal about herself, her family and Hyatt, "the poor young writer" who played such a large part in her thoughts. She trusted him enough to invite him to Enfield to give a lecture to a local society. She even told him about her unhappy teaching days, and begged a clerkship in his bank for a former pupil. The young man responded to this kindness by absconding with some money, causing Florence intense misery and self reproach.[19] Clodd kindly assured her that she was not to blame, but she later confessed that she had *never* tried to be exceptionally kind without being bitterly disappointed afterwards. The memory of these trustful confidences was all the more distressing when Clodd, proposing to write his memoirs, ceased to be "dear, kind Mr. Clodd" and the cheerful, gossipy house at Aldeburgh appeared "a trap" in which she had risked her reputation. In fact Clodd wrote of his friends so kindly and discreetly as to be almost boring, but Florence was hypersensitive even to imaginary slights or dangers.

In April 1910, briefly, she achieved a long-standing ambition; a woman friend who was going abroad lent her a small flat in the West End, in a mansion block near Baker Street station. Here Florence could write without domestic interruptions and feel herself, at the age of thirty-one, an independent career woman. Here Florence invited her married sister, Ethel Richardson, with her little son, "to meet Mr. Hardy". Hardy took Florence's nephew on his knee and asked him kindly "what he wanted to be when he was a man". The little boy of six, who had just been to Kew Gardens with their huge and fascinating greenhouses, promptly replied "a gardener". From that time, wrote Florence's sister, "there were occasional meetings with T.H. when he was in London". She does not mention that other members of the family knew the great man, but she would hardly have taken her little boy to meet him unless Hardy's friendship with Florence had appeared perfectly proper to the Dugdales.[20]

Florence used this flat for one more attempt at journalism, this time as a freelance contributor to the *Evening Standard*. Inevitably the introduction came through Hardy. The paper wanted to interview him on his seventieth birthday, but he would not consent to this. Instead he agreed to an article "written by my secretary, Miss Dugdale". "The fact is," explained Hardy rather unnecessarily to Clodd, "I knew they would print *something* and I preferred to fall into her hands ... as I know I can always depend on her good taste."[21] The article appeared unsigned under the heading "Our Greatest Writer"; it has a double interest as representing Florence's view of Hardy, endorsed by himself. Like all her published writing, it is conscientious, careful and correct; the manuscript was submitted to Hardy before she handed it in, and probably subjected to his usual judicious touching up, for the "good taste" is conspicuous.[22]

The article stressed various points on which Hardy felt he had been misrepresented or misunderstood by the general public. The writer hoped and believed that he would spend his birthday "cheerfully," refuting the charge of pessimism. "Mr Hardy is not, as might be expected by readers of his books, tired of life and the world." Rather unexpectedly, Florence chose to mention his interest in picture galleries; since she herself was an enthusiastic visitor to the National Gallery, it may be that they found this a convenient, anonymous meeting place. She mentioned his civic service as a magistrate, and his consistent stand against "cruelty and oppression". A love and sympathy for defenceless animals was certainly one of the bonds between her and Hardy, as it had been between him and Emma. The article referred tactfully to his agnosticism, without attacking religion; "Mr. Hardy has ever looked beyond the puppet to the elemental pulling the strings." It emphasized what was essential to Hardy, the importance he attached to his poetry; he "is now a poet having returned to his earlier love and forsaken prose fiction". Implicitly the admirers who plagued him "to return to novel writing" were rebuked. The article ended with a tribute to the one work by Hardy in which Florence could feel she had played, however humbly, her own part. "Mr. Hardy has written one long work in mingled prose and verse which may be considered by another generation the cream and summit of his literary labours. The novels may fade in the resplendence of *The Dynasts*, in which the spirit as well as the events of a whole era of English and continental history is given with amazing power and truth of detail. Mr. Hardy is a great writer, perhaps greater than his generation knows."

The *Standard* editors were "much pleased" with this article, as well they might be, since Hardy notoriously disliked publicity; they asked if Miss Dugdale could provide any "similar sketches". It is hard not to feel that she was known in Fleet Street, as someone who commanded Hardy's influence and patronage. He at once wrote off from the Athenaeum, requesting an interview for Florence with Edward Clodd, on his impending seventieth birthday. If Clodd would call, "she would jot down a few notes ... what they particularly want is *anecdote* etc. in which you are so rich".[23] Clodd, though fond of Florence, did not share Hardy's overwhelming enthusiasm for her literary talents; he felt privately, "I honestly don't care about it", but, kind as ever, agreed. When he saw the typescript he was dismayed and "begged her not to print. This craving for details is unwholesome." Florence printed her article, "but happily the purple patches all left out, so I breathe more freely".[24] The interview for this article had been a long "chat" at the Lyceum Club, where Clodd called on 23 June 1910. Their conversation predictably worked round to the Hardys. Towards Hardy himself, Florence's feelings were subtly changing. She still believed, as she had written, "none can deny that he is the greatest writer left to England". Yet as a character, he no longer commanded the breathless awe of the young schoolteacher that Florence had been five years before. Through meeting him, she had come to see much more of the world and formed new standards of comparison.

For some weeks Florence continued to attempt a freelance career. She may have written a brief article on Hardy's Order of Merit, since she was said to "do work" for the *Evening Standard*, though as the article was unsigned this remains merely an inference.[25] She was also said to have written for the *Daily Mail*, but these unsigned contributions cannot be traced with any conviction. It is impossible to say if her contributions continued when the flat had to be given up and she returned to Enfield. Florence was hardly tough enough in body or mind to hold her own in the free-for-all of newspaper work, and without Hardy's determination to launch her, it seems doubtful whether she would have made the attempt.

In any case her life was about to enter a new phase. Among the lady members of the Lyceum Club, with their literary aspirations, was that thwarted but determined author, Emma Lavinia Hardy, who in June 1910 gave a lecture at the club. Afterwards Florence was introduced, possibly by Dora Shorter, to Mrs. Hardy, who by all the evidence seems to have been unaware of her existence until this time. Florence, schooled in tact, immediately endeared herself by praising the lecture, which she offered to type. Emma took an immediate fancy to this fragile young woman, so unlike the society hostesses who snubbed her and made her husband, she believed, "vain and selfish".[26] The Hardys had rented a flat in Maida Vale for the season, where Emma would give her usual afternoon "at homes", which the painter Jacques-Emile Blanche found so pathetically dowdy and provincial. Not so Florence, who declared it "a pleasure and an honour" to be asked. "I shall be delighted to pour out tea for you on Thursday afternoon. I will be at your flat at four o'clock, but could be earlier if there were anything you wished me to do beforehand."[27] Helpful, deferential and skilled as a social companion, Florence made an excellent impression. Before June was out, she had been invited by Emma to spend a week at Max Gate.[28]

Five days after her first letter to Mrs. Hardy, Florence had a long talk with Edward Clodd at the Lyceum Club. "She had much to say," wrote Clodd, "re Hardy et uxor." Meeting the warm-hearted Emma had changed her feelings towards Hardy, whom she found somewhat unfair to his wife; "he is a great writer, but not a great man". It is not clear whether Emma or Florence herself first delivered this pithy judgment. Evidently, though, it stuck in Clodd's memory, for eighteen years later, at Hardy's death, he was to reproduce it as his own.[29]

7

"Mute Ministrations"

THE ATMOSPHERE of summer days in house and garden at Max Gate during July 1910 is touchingly captured in Hardy's poem *After the Visit.*

> Come again, with the feet
> That were light on the green as a thistledown ball,
> And those mute ministrations to one and to all
> Beyond a man's saying sweet.
>
> Until then the faint scent
> Of the bordering flowers swam unheeded away,
> And I marked not the charm in the changes of day
> As the cloud-colours came and went.

The poem was first printed in the *Spectator* of 13 August 1910, though, of course, without its dedication "To F.E.D.". Yet Florence was well aware that she had inspired the poem, for she had her own personal copy, which she had already shown to Clodd. "F.D.", he wrote on 8 August, five days before *After the Visit* was published, "sent me to read a poem addressed to her by T.H. after her visit to him."[1] Few emotions are more sad than sexual love across the generations; if Florence had shared the poignant tenderness of this poem, she would surely not have wanted to display it to a third party. Indeed in another poem, *Had You Wept*, Hardy wistfully reproaches a woman who shows no "passionate need for clinging" or sign of responding to his grief at what cannot be. Perhaps her situation was simply too strange for Florence to comprehend.

Whatever she, or Hardy in the depths of his reticent heart, may have felt, the once-masterful Mrs. Hardy took possession of her in everyday life. Elderly, myopic and muddled, she seems to have felt that charming, "useful" Miss Dugdale was her personal discovery. Florence was freely admitted to the household where, since the publication of *Jude the Obscure* in 1895, the Hardys had existed in bitter, ill-concealed hostility. Emma seized on this new compliant listener for a recital of her old grievance about Hardy's neglect of her career as a novelist. Florence, whose own work Hardy had stage-managed so tirelessly, found herself enlisted in a bizarre alliance with his wife. At first the Max Gate ménage "wore an air of comedy".

After superb Ely House the red-brick villa, entered through a tunnel of privet, the dark rooms with portraits of Emma's glowering Gifford relatives, the shrouding plush tablecloths and crochet anti-macassars, the patches of damp and discolouration on the walls, seemed disillusioning to a degree.[2] Local society Florence found thoroughly provincial with "no mental companionship" for a writer. Emma herself, her "Protestant principles", her pampered cats allowed to sleep on the dinner-wagon, her dark suspicions that Hardy resembled the wife-murderer Dr. Crippen, was an irresistible figure of fun. Yet, as so many people found, Emma's genuine kindness was overwhelming. "Mrs. Hardy is good to me beyond words," wrote Florence truthfully to Clodd. "I am *intensely* sorry for her, sorry indeed for both."[3]

"Thank you so much for all your goodness to me," wrote Florence to Emma after her first visit. "I feel I cannot find words sufficient to thank you for your great kindness." In October she wrote," The days I spend at Max Gate are all so happy that I sometimes fear I shall be spoiled for the sterner realities of life."[4] In November 1910 Mrs. Dugdale fell ill and Emma at once sent off "a beautiful pheasant which arrived safely" at 5 River Front. When Emma herself fell ill and went home to Dorchester, leaving Hardy alone in London, she confidently trusted Florence to call as often as possible and oversee his housekeeping.[5] The two ladies found further common ground as aspiring authors. Florence rashly promised help in "the great campaign which lies before us", to place Mrs. Hardy's long neglected manuscripts. When she read one of Emma's tracts aloud, her mother "found it most beautiful and comforting ... I shall try to find some good publisher who publishes religious works."[6] She "roused the publisher's curiosity by telling him it was written by a well-known lady, a philanthropist and writer", but, alas, by the end of August "had heard nothing more from the publisher".[7] Florence re-typed Emma's thirty-year-old short novel, *The Maid on the Shore*, with tactful advice from her fashion-writing experience. "Certain *costumes* are described fully and these—appropriate as they must have been when the story was written—would only make the story seem ridiculous now." She tried to keep up Emma's hopes about the religious pieces. "I am just burning with anxiety to know the fate of *The Acceptors*. I fancy though that your great triumph will be with *The Inspirer*."[8] The theme of this last story was, most pathetically, "a wife who *inspired* her husband's novels";[9] it had been rejected a dozen years back. By October 1910, even Florence was forced to sound a warning note. "I am afraid there will be no *financial* gain in publishing this—because the highest forms of literature seem rarely to have any great commercial value." In despair she suggested the *Hibbert Journal*, but in November admitted "an unpleasant rebuff concerning *The Acceptors* ... We *must* accomplish something ... Perhaps the stories are hardly modern enough, though exquisitely written." To comfort Emma, Florence suggested collaborating in a play. "I have been able to think of no good *plot* ... some strong *situations* must be introduced ... as you say we will not be discouraged but press on steadily."[10] Kindly, she dwelt on her own failings as a novelist. "I am just finishing a chapter and in looking over it, I find there is absolutely no conversation. Although the psychological style is in vogue now, I fancy bright and sparkling conversation is needed." By December, "the publishers are doing nothing until they have all their Christmas books out". In the end, to Hardy's considerable embarrassment, Emma had some of her poems printed and bound by a Dorchester firm. Yet Florence's rash encouragement did in the end achieve something of value. She persuaded the older woman "to finish off the reminiscences",[11] the notebook containing the naive, yet almost poetic *Some Recollections*, which form Emma's best and only memorial. Ironically, the reading of them after Emma's death was to inspire many of the exquisite poems to his dead wife which wounded Hardy's young second wife so deeply.

In letters to Edward Clodd, who had established himself as her confidant, Florence described life at Max Gate with a frankness she afterwards came to regret. Always hungry for the friendship of cultured people, she responded with ardent indiscretion to offers of sympathy. "I do *hope* you burn my letters!" she exclaimed to a later friend.[12] Clodd showed gratifying interest; "story of more ructions in the Hardy ménage," he noted,[13] after a chance meeting with Florence in London. He liked to "chaff" the Olympian Hardy, and the two of them made mild fun of the great man's hypochondria, his self-absorption, his inveterate stinginess, so noticeable after the Stokers' generosity, and above all his tendency to "luxuriate in misery". November 1910 was to show two characters in sharp contrast. Hardy shut himself up in his study to write a melancholy poem on the burial of his white study cat in the Max Gate pets' necropolis: "that little white cat was his only friend".[14] Soon after, while the sale at Ely House was actually in progress, came a telegram to tell Florence "my dear, dear friend Lady Stoker died of pneumonia ... I have told you of my good and kind friend in Dublin," Florence reminded Clodd; "he has had another, a more crushing blow. His wife, Lady Stoker, died last night. In the face of such a calamity, I cannot write and sympathize very deeply with T.H. upon the death of Kitsey."[15] As the death certificate testifies, Sir Thornley Stoker was with his wife at her death in the nursing-home to which she had been moved; to protect her to the last, her funeral was entirely private.

8   Florence at Max Gate drawn by William Strang, 26 September 1910

Florence continued to live at home with her family and the literary circle surrounding Alfred Hyatt. She may have wanted to maintain her independence; yet on repeated visits, she was being drawn steadily into the web of the Hardys' lives. She told Clodd that Mrs. Hardy, "instead of cooling towards me grows more and more affectionate".[16] There was a strange scene on 26 September, when the artist William Strang came to Max Gate to draw an official portrait of Hardy as a member of the Order of Merit. He may have been mildly surprised to be asked for a portrait of the author's secretary; however he made and dedicated the drawing on the spot, capturing Florence's fine, melancholy features and the great luminous grey eyes which Hardy loved. It remained Florence's favourite likeness of herself.[17] Another link was made when she visited Hardy's brother and sisters, usually carefully hidden from curious visitors such as Clement Shorter, who might be tempted to "get copy" from their simplicity.[18] Florence came to love kind, Dorset-speaking Henry, "a Gabriel Oak or a Giles Winterborne", Mary, who adored her famous brother, and jolly Kate. The three schoolteachers must have found common ground, for Florence reported to Clodd that Hardy's mysterious sisters were "ladylike, refined and well-informed",[19] although since a quarrel with Emma they were not received at Max Gate. Returning to Enfield, she sent them each a postcard because they had asked kindly about her home. The conventional messages reveal her ingrained diffidence. "This is Enfield. It is not so pretty as Dorchester and of course not nearly so sweet as Bockhampton—but still it might be worse." Another picture carried the sad little message, "You see we have a few green nooks in Enfield although it is terribly suburban in parts."[20]

At Max Gate, it seemed strangely as though both the Hardys were in love with this girl, so much younger than their withered embittered selves. November brought Emma's birthday which, according to Florence, Hardy always forgot. She gave the older woman "a small present of pink candle-shades from Selfridges", wishing her affectionately "years full of sunshine, prosperity and every happiness". On the current suffrage question, the two women appeared to differ. Emma subscribed to the London Society for Women's Suffrage and indeed donated "an old-style Brocade Dress" to be worn in processions. She was prepared for a long struggle: "Men's *power* and OBSTINACY being exceedingly great."

Then in June 1910, when Emma and Florence were first meeting, a comic misunderstanding occurred. Emma objected to "violent acts of stonethrowing etc by the *suffragettes*". Yet a lady called, who "asserted in a most ill-bred manner that Mrs. Hardy had previously belonged to the militant set, which she certainly does not and would abhor to belong to and had worn the wrong colours which probably inadvertantly she *had* some very long time since".[21] Much tact was needed to sort out the muddle and soothe Emma's ruffled feelings. Florence had a narrow escape from the suffragettes, of whom she had written so critically in *The Sphere*, only to fall into the arms of Emma's anti-ritualists. "Nearly her whole attention", wrote Mrs. Hardy of herself, "is given to the Protestant cause, the whole situation being in such a critical condition by the aggressive attempt of the R. C. Hierarchy to interfere with our simple services and subvert free, flourishing England and aggressive attitude of the *Roman Cs.*"[22] When Florence was at home in Enfield, Emma pursued her with "Protestant Papers" and enquires after her "Protestant Bible Class". Florence responded with little parcels for an Evangelical Bazaar and outrage over High Church appointments: "with treachery like that within the Church of England, how can we resist the deadly attacks of Rome? Those men are *virtually Romanists!*"[23] Next Mrs. Hardy began to plan a lengthy stay in France, which Florence encouraged, "until she told me that she wanted *me* to go with her!"[24] In a series of transparent letters about bitter cold, unheated French houses, and friends who caught pneumonia and nearly died at Boulogne, Florence wriggled out of it. The life of a lady companion was hard; like any young woman, she must sometimes have longed for an escape and a life of her own.

She spent Christmas 1910 at Enfield, and later said she remembered it above all other Christmases, perhaps because it was to be the last Christmas in her friend Hyatt's life. He looked "far from robust", but continued to work on a series of anthologies from French sources; during 1911 he produced volumes on Madame de Sévigné, La Rochefoucauld and George Sand. Was it to help him that Florence attended French classes this winter?[25] Nor did she forget other friends. She wrote regularly to Sir Thornley Stoker, and heard about the great sale in which, during one week, the collections of forty years were broken up and scattered. All that remained of the splendours of Ely House was the auctioneer's illustrated catalogue, price 2/6. Stoker left the home he had restored with such imaginative skill and moved to a smaller town house in Hatch Street.[26] It was probably now that he gave Florence an antique ring, from among those in the sale, choosing with innate tact not a gem stone, but a classical engraving of the second century B.C. on amethyst, which became, until it was stolen, one of her most prized possessions.[27] Like all Sir Thornley's friends, she hoped that now the long tragedy of his wife's illness was over, he would begin a new and happy life. He said nothing to discourage this idea, but began quietly putting his affairs in order. He knew from his clinical experience that he had not long to live, and prepared to die as he had lived, with consideration for others and a certain elegance. Florence does not mention that she ever visited or saw him again, but time would show that he had not forgotten her.

In the New Year of 1911, Florence escaped from Emma's possessive affection to a new post. Already before Christmas Hardy had introduced her to a sympathetic friend in London, as "by far the most interesting type of femininity the world provides for men's

eyes", which the friend interpreted as meaning "a modern, emancipated young woman of cities".[28] This friend, the Hon. Mrs. Henniker,
was Florence's ideal, an intelligent, spirited, charming society
woman, "always ready to be amused". Hardy had been seriously
in love with her during the 1890s and though she deftly cooled his
wilder hopes, had continued to forward her career as a society novelist, with much greater success than poor Florence achieved. Now,
for old friendship's sake, Mrs. Henniker welcomed the struggling
young writer to Stratford Place, where she kept open house to
fashionable and literary London. "*Nobody* but you does kind things
like that," wrote Hardy, shedding his reserve. "I am so glad you
like her; she quite loves you."[29] Florence Henniker's kindness, part
of her easy, elegant charm, extended to everyone around her; her
ladies' maid became a much loved friend who stayed with her for
forty years. "She was beautiful and gifted and the kindest friend
one could conceive," wrote Florence, who inevitably came to feel
herself one of the family. She typed Mrs. Henniker's stories, admired
large, benevolent Major-General Henniker, and took their French
bulldogs, Milner and Empire, for runs in the park. She accompanied Mrs. Henniker on visits to her brother Lord Crewe, a former
Lord Lieutenant of Ireland, who had knighted Thornley Stoker.
Mrs. Henniker, of course, knew the Stokers and Ely House. Florence,
enchanted, told tolerant, unshockable Mrs. Henniker "every detail
of my life and she entered into it as a sister ... I went to see her
frequently and could use her house as a hotel practically whenever
I liked."[30] When there was no typing to do, Mrs. Henniker kindly
invited her "to run up to have lunch and go to a matinée". Her
own conversation was as good as a theatre, for she was the daughter
of Keats's first biographer, the legendary Victorian host Monckton
Milnes. She could remember going for a carriage drive with Thackeray, who made up nonsense rhymes for her, when she was four years
old. Swinburne had played croquet with her, Dickens was an old
friend, Thiers had taken her in to dinner at Versailles. All this she
related casually, with careless generosity, as she shared her interesting guests.[31] "The people she had there were all so interesting,"
Florence recalled with vague yearnings, "so delightful, writers,
soldiers, politicians ... one never met any *dull* person there". The
atmosphere went to her head, as once it had to Hardy's; she roamed
the grand Mayfair house "as if it were my home, almost",[32] with
daydreams of a literary salon of her own.

Hardy wrote to Florence on 11 January 1911, and though he seldom left Max Gate in winter, came to London to visit his "young
friend". Florence joked to Clodd that Hardy had "a sore throat and
it's my fault, because I make him talk in the street and then germs
attack him. He was taking germ-killers the whole time too." She

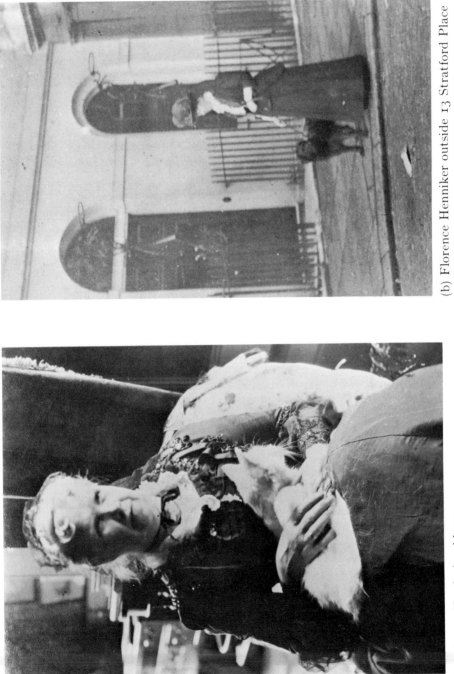

(a) Emma Hardy in old age

(b) Florence Henniker outside 13 Stratford Place

9 Two employers

also ridiculed his plans to rent an economical flat for the London season in dingy Finsbury Park.[33] Yet Hardy had come for her sake, to negotiate with the editor of the *Cornhill*, who printed in his February 1911 number a second story signed F. E. Dugdale. This was *Blue Jimmy*, a three-thousand-word factual account of a real thief, who stole a horse from Hardy's own Higher Bockhampton Lane and was hanged in a Somerset gaol. This story is entirely in Hardy's style, while the proof copy is corrected and expanded entirely in his handwriting. Hardy had "improved" the work of all his literary ladies, but this went further. It is impossible to say what drove the two to such a step; one can only feel very sorry for both.

Fortunately, Florence also had an independent commission in 1911 and 1912, to write some "little stories about birds and animals" for the Oxford University Press. These were to accompany pictures by the distinguished animal artist E. J. Detmold. She went to work with her usual conscientious thoroughness, producing not stories but careful informative descriptions of animals and birds. *The Book of Baby Beasts* came out in 1911 and *The Book of Baby Birds* the following year. They are essentially art books, half-folio size, on heavy paper, with illustrations beautifully printed, in a linen-like mount. Detmold's pictures were water-colours in the Japanese manner, minutely detailed yet austere, for example, one magpie on a single pine branch. Beside the distinction of these studies any text might appear commonplace; Florence's "stories" are a series of natural history lessons, revealing the efficient teacher she had been. "It was before the dawn of history, long ages ago, that the Dog was first domesticated by man. Today he is our most faithful servant and companion." The most sympathetic accounts were of small wild creatures, like the squirrel, sleeping through the winter with fluffy tail wrapped round him as a blanket. Verse was not Florence's forte. The unsigned poems Hardy contributed—the Calf, the Yellowhammer, the Fawn, the Kitten—stand out from the rest. The text remained subordinate to the illustrations, and was omitted when Detmold's plates were re-issued in the 1920s.

By early spring 1911, Hardy was worrying about Florence's usual winter colds and hoping for the usual visit to Aldeburgh, where "the sea revives her wonderfully". Clodd, always hospitable, responded and on 8 April 1911,[34] Hardy met Florence's train from Enfield and escorted her across Liverpool Street station, to "run down" to Aldeburgh. "Two or three days of your air does pick her up so."[35] Persistent ill-health seemed, strangely, part of Florence's charm for him. Another engagement could no longer be put off; in July Florence went for her long-promised holiday with Mrs. Hardy. Emma's defiant cheerfulness and gusto were slowly being worn down by age and painful illness, the impacted gall-stones which eventually caused her death. She spoke of feeling Continental at heart, as befitted the Bohemian author she still pathetically believed herself to be; but she was forced to settle for two weeks with Florence at "Wavecrest", 6 New Parade, Worthing, during exceptionally fine weather in July and August. The holiday-makers were photographed on the beach, Florence and a friend as rather coy bathing belles, Emma, a black bombazine Canute, repelling the sunshine with a large umbrella. Florence wrote a card to Mary Hardy in familiar terms. "This card shows the house where I have been staying and the road I cross daily in my bathing dress."[36] Hardy recorded in his *Life*: "in July Mrs. Hardy accompanied by her friend Miss Florence Dugdale went to stay in Worthing," a passage that Florence, with feelings one can only imagine, later cancelled in the typescript.[37] In October, Florence made a brief visit to Weymouth, where Hardy, as he told sympathetic Mrs. Henniker, was "going to run down this afternoon to see how she is getting on".[38] In December they made a brief excursion to the West Country, well chaperoned by Kate Hardy. They had settled into a routine, painful perhaps to Hardy but quite satisfactory from Florence's point of view, of discreet, public meetings.

   The emotional centre of Florence's life still lay where it had been for so many years, at home in Enfield. Then, returning from the West Country trip, she found news which brought deep grief and distress. On 9 December 1911, while she had been away, Alfred Hyatt had died. A week before, though looking frail and ill, he had been out and about his work as a local journalist, when he suffered a sudden haemorrhage. Overworked and weakened by years of illness, he had little resistance: his lungs collapsed and he died swiftly. He was forty years old.[39] At first Florence could hardly believe it. "That poor young writer of whom I wrote died yesterday," she told Clodd. "I had not expected so speedy an end . . . I think his last days were brightened by the hope that *something* might be done for him."[40] Since she was twenty he had been "more to me than anything else in the world", close in age, in family background, in tastes and beliefs, the one person with whom she could be simply herself. No ambition to rise in the world could outweigh that old affection. Now, she later said, she felt a desolate loneliness: "the feeling that there is no one much in the world who cares whether I am happy or sad. It is of all feelings the worst." Marriage and social success, when it came, did little to ease this loss; she said she would "gladly have given the rest of her life for one brief half-hour" with her dead love.[41] Nothing could take the place of this unknown journalist, dying in his suburban room. It was a sad, a Hardyesque irony.

8

"From Youth to Dreary Middle-Age"

HYATT'S BURIAL, to which Florence sent a wreath, began a year of deaths; the cast and setting of her life changed swiftly, like a transformation scene in some melancholy theatre. She fell into the mood which surviving acquaintances still remember, kind, generous, yet with an overshadowing sadness. The first to vanish, on 6 February 1912, was Major-General Henniker; ironically he had commanded a battalion through the Boer War, to die now of heart-failure after being kicked by a horse. Mrs. Henniker, who liked funerals to be "as simple and cheerful as possible, with no mourning of the slightest kind", buried him quietly at his family home in Suffolk. She had loved her soldier husband through thirty years of marriage and the hospitable house in Stratford Place was sad without him. Florence Dugdale stayed with her to help compile "a little book for his friends", and the two women, so different in background, yet both mourning a loss, grew very close to one another. "She has a beautiful nature, very full of sympathy," wrote Mrs. Henniker of Florence; and Hardy agreed: "As you say, she is very sympathetic—so much so that her own health is largely dependent on the happiness or otherwise of her friends."[1] He admitted that he had written some verses for the General's memoir because "dear F.D." begged him to. "She assured me you would like them."[2]

Sympathy for Mrs. Henniker was tinged with wistful regret. Florence was so unhappy during these months, that for once in her life she felt a hunger for the comfort of religious faith. Unlike her earlier employers, Mrs. Henniker was a High Churchwoman, who could offer prayers for her dead husband at the church where she worshipped, St. Anselm's, Davies Street. Florence, longing for consolation, had serious talks with a Roman Catholic priest,[3] probably Father Thomas Dawson, who had married the Shorters and was a close friend of their household. Seeing her distraught condition, he scrupulously made no attempt to influence her, and she came to look back on this with mingled relief and regret. Summer brought another grief, for which she was ill-prepared. At Whitsuntide she had received a letter from Sir Thornley Stoker, saying that he had been unwell but she was not to worry as he would soon be better.[4] Privately, he told former colleagues that he had arterio-sclerosis and increasing cardiac weakness; he was only sixty-seven, but he had

poured out his strength for patients, students and his sick wife. Death
soon came to him, wrote a friend, "gradually, painlessly and peacefully, as sleep to a child", leaving "honour, love and troops of
friends".[5] He was mourned by the whole of medical Dublin, though
by no one so much as the patients in the poor law wards whom he
had treated with such invariable kindness and courtesy. In July
1912, when his will was proved, apart from bequests to nieces and
nephews, he had left substantial legacies, five thousand pounds to
his wife's nurse Miss Webb and two thousand pounds to Florence
Dugdale.[6] This sum, worth well over ten times as much in present-
day values, infuriated the chronically hard-up Bram Stoker family,
who referred to Florence as "that woman who got the Stoker
money". They maintained that she had been Sir Thornley's mistress,
"under the cover of being a secretary".[7] There is not an iota of evidence for this, and it seems probable that, like the irreproachable
Miss Webb, Florence was being rewarded for kindness to the invalid
Lady Stoker.

Sir Thornley's kindness had given Florence security, freedom
from money worries and an independence she had never known
before. Nothing shows her generous side more clearly than the first
use she made of this bequest. Remembering her own early struggles,
she sent her youngest sister to college for three years[8] to take a
domestic science qualification; for this sister, fifteen years younger
than herself, she had an almost maternal affection. Florence was now
free from the need to take a resident post and could devote herself
entirely to writing; yet there was nowhere she particularly wanted
to go and depression continued to haunt her. "I feel so little zest
for life," she complained. A former pupil remembers postcards and
letters from the Sussex coast, where she went for holidays in an
attempt to revive her health.[9]

For much of 1912 Florence was at home in her parents' house,
writing. The play and the psychological novel were apparently abandoned and forgotten; instead she produced the best work of her life,
In Lucy's Garden.[10] The idea of a children's garden book may have
owed something to the success of F. Hodgson Burnett's *The Secret
Garden*, published in 1911, but Florence's plan and content were
drawn from an earlier model, Hyatt's *From a Middlesex Garden*,
written ten years earlier, in the early days of their own relationship.
Like him, Florence traces the year round in a single garden, but in
her book the process is seen through a child's eyes. Lucy lives in
a dignified old house with a spacious walled garden, very like the
Gentlemans' Row houses which Florence had admired in her own
childhood. Lucy goes into the January garden to feed the hungry
birds; "the iron roller which kept the paths smooth had a cap of
snow and the forked branches of the old apple tree each held a downy

handful". In March she sows; "she held the little brown seeds for a long while and looked at them before she scattered them in the earth". In spring she climbs on the garden wall; "weather had darkened the bricks and little green cushions of moss grew between them on the mortar, but Lucy was sure the wall did not mind growing old". Here Lucy meets Peter, who is staying with his grandmother next door. They play robbers and pirates, watch snails together, an unconventional touch, and make a private post office in a hollow tree. In summer, Lucy arranges a tea-party for dolls on the soft green orchard grass, but a black and white cat arrives uninvited and puts his paws on the tablecloth, perhaps a memory of the visiting cats who frequented Emma's garden tea-parties at Max Gate,[11] to the surprise of literary visitors. In September, as the apples ripen, Lucy has a dream of Pomona the Apple Queen, which exactly reflects Hyatt's September and Pomona passages. In autumn gales, Lucy's mother gently comforts the two children, by telling them how the wind returns the leaves to mother earth, so they "may again become green leaves, beautiful flowers or rich fruit". Perhaps it was herself Florence Dugdale was comforting, for clearly she is Lucy's mother, gentle, serious and well-informed. The old house and walled garden are the home she would have loved and Lucy and Peter the lively, affectionate children she would never have. She had been inspired by loss; *In Lucy's Garden* is a charming book, a little sentimental in its period style, but fresh and full of feeling. It is also, perhaps, as close as we shall ever come to Florence's essential character.

Apart from the usual two meetings at Aldeburgh, Florence does not seem to have seen a great deal of Hardy during 1912. Perhaps the Hardys' fixed resentments were more than her depression could face, for Hardy complained rather sadly that she had not visited Max Gate for a long time.[12] Thanks to Sir Thornley's legacy, she was no longer obliged to attend as companion or secretary. By one of the ironies which seemed to gather round Hardy, Florence made her long-delayed visit to see the Hardy Players perform *The Trumpet Major* on 27 November 1912. Florence arrived at Weymouth, where she was staying "for the sea air" and was met by a telegram which sent her hurrying to Max Gate. Emma had died, with Hardy bending over her, at eight o'clock that morning. In this crisis, Florence at once moved in to his house, rather to the resentment of the dead woman's servants.[13] Looking back in later years, Florence came to see this date, which had started as a commonplace day like any other, as the watershed of her life. "On that day I seemed suddenly to leap from youth to dreary middle-age. I suppose because I had no responsibility before."[14]

After a few days Florence went home, but Hardy needed her "to help me with the proofs of the American edition of my book which happen to be in full swing".[15] She returned to Max Gate to find Emma's niece Lilian Gifford "attending to the house affairs" and the ill-assorted ménage-à-trois spent Christmas together. Lilian was a pathetic figure, a lonely spinster clinging to the memory of the aunt, who had brought her up so kindly, and resenting Florence as an interloper. "She is imbued", Florence told Clodd, "with ideas of the grandeur of the Gifford family and the great Archdeacon and the vulgarity of Mr. Hardy's relatives and she insists, too, that Mr. Hardy would *never* have been a great writer, had it not been for 'dear Aunt's influence'."[16] She fled to Enfield, where Clodd was to give a lecture to a literary society, when she confided that Hardy was promising to send Lilian away and pleading with her to return. In the New Year of 1913, Florence made the decisive move of her life. She returned to take charge at Max Gate, a responsibility she was to carry without respite for as long as Hardy lived.

Her first impression never really altered; "life here is *lonely* beyond words". She took as much care of Hardy as she possibly could, read aloud to him every evening after dinner until eleven o'clock and walked with him on his only outings to Stinsford churchyard. Both were perhaps uneasy in their new relationship. Hardy wanted to hide Florence, because "you know what people are like in a small town like Dorchester and how they talk ... if it is known that I am staying at Max Gate they will comment unpleasantly".[17] Clodd expressed sympathy, though privately he thought this agitation "rather small beer". His comment on the death of Emma had been confident, if mistaken. "*Death of Mrs Hardy*," he had confided to his diary on 27 November; "he'll feel relief at this." Meanwhile he continued to receive Florence's rather breathless confidences. "I ought not to write all this I know, but it is a most tremendous relief to do so and I know you won't ever breathe a *word* to anyone."[18]

Hardy too must have felt the strain, for he drafted, on paper watermarked 1913,[19] a lyric *In the Street*, which describes his suffering when they are forced to meet in public as strangers;

> But far, near, left and right,
> Here or there,
> By day or dingiest night,
> Everywhere
> I see you: one incomparably fair!
>
> So do we wend our ways,
> Beautiful girl,
> Along our parallel days:
> While unfurl
> Our futures and what there may whelm and whirl.

He refused to allow Florence to be seen with him in the streets of Dorchester and from this time dates the hatred of journalists, which was to be such a feature of their lives together. These precautions were useless, for, of course, the existence of Florence could not be hidden. The resentful Max Gate servants reported that she was Hardy's mistress, and in Dorchester well-brought-up girls were not allowed to speak to him.[20] Such indignation was largely beside the point, for Hardy was seventy-three and Florence depressed and ailing; moreover she was conscious of "a lack of real feeling on my part" for sex and love-making. This was hardly the centre of their lives.

Far more important, now and always, was the shift in their emotional relationship. For Emma, in life a figure of fun or pity, had become by the mysterious alchemy of death a potent and unassailable rival. Hardy plunged into the series of passionately grieving poems to his lost wife, which as *Poems of 1912–1913* occur in his most famous poetic volume. Nothing was real to him but the source of his inspiration, and he clearly had no thought to spare for Florence's feelings. For she, knowing the realities of the Hardys' later life together, was bewildered. She had always dreamt of the literary life, as she understood it; now she experienced the ruthlessness of the creative artist at work. In March, Hardy set off with his brother Henry on a pilgrimage to the scenes of his first meeting with Emma more than forty years ago, before Florence was even born, in a world from which she must be for ever excluded. She was left behind in cold, damp Max Gate, where encircling trees shut out the light and wet leaves blew against the window panes. "It is very quiet and lonely here," she wrote, "and I keep a loaded revolver in my bedroom ... Having no one to talk to, it is a relief to be able to write."[21] No one was really to blame; but it was a sad life.

Florence had been trained from childhood to submit to authority. She endured the dark shadow Hardy's memories cast across her life in silence; yet inwardly she rebelled. "I feel I can hardly keep back my true opinion much longer," she told Clodd, within a month of Emma's death. She described Hardy's shock on finding the "diabolical diaries" which the unhappy Emma had filled with hatred and abuse of her husband to within a few days of her death. Hardy dismissed them as "sheer hallucination in her, poor thing", and told Clodd Emma had latterly believed she was being followed, because "people were conspiring against her".[22] "All I hope", wrote Florence with uncomfortable prescience after three months at Max Gate, "is that I may not, for the rest of his life, have to sit and listen humbly to an account of her virtues and graces."[23] From the time of finding the diaries, her old pity and affection for Emma turned to a lasting revulsion.

Florence's friends, Clodd, the Shorters, Mrs. Henniker, were worried by her compromising situation at Max Gate, though her parents, with dignified reticence, have left no hint of their opinions on their daughter's private life. Hardy felt they must not be seen together in public. "Mr Hardy's regard for appearances", explained Florence to Clodd, "will decide that I *mustn't* go to Aldeburgh with him for a twelvemonth or so."[24] Mrs. Henniker, kind as always, invited Florence to stay in a seaside house she had rented at Southwold, and in April Hardy visited them there.[25] Later Florence "confided a great secret" to the ever-interested Clodd. If this was a proposal of marriage, Hardy had made it in his own manner, taking the pretty young woman of thirty-four to Stinsford churchyard, where among the graves of Emma and his relations, he had selected a corner "reserved for me". All through 1913, Florence's sensitive temperament seems to have wavered painfully to and fro. Sometimes she felt she had never fully appreciated Hardy, "the depth of his affection and his goodness and unselfishness". She was touched to hear Kate say he had his youthful, happy laugh again. At other times she felt a revulsion from his prevailing gloom. "He has had cartloads of sympathy (mostly insincere) and I cannot see that anyone—dead or alive—is the better off for him being miserable."[26]

The past forced its way painfully into everyday life. It was difficult to introduce visitors; Shorter's journalistic habit of asking "all sorts of questions", for instance, made Hardy "almost frantic".[27] Yet after some delay, on 11 July 1913, Clodd and Shorter came for the weekend. As well as the usual sights, Admiral Hardy's monument and Maiden Castle, they visited the scenes of Hardy's past life: Emma's grave at Stinsford by his wish, and the romantic thatched cottage at Higher Bockhampton where he had been born. Hardy talked of his mother and of his apprenticeship to a Dorchester architect in the 1850s, long before Florence existed. On Sunday afternoon, the curious Clodd met Hardy's brother and sisters for the first time. He learnt of the family quarrel with Emma. "She even accused Katie Hardy of stealing a pair of earrings and Hardy looked on while she sent for the Police. 'Tis a shame he did not let me know these good folk earlier. He should be proud of them," wrote Clodd indignantly.[28] These grotesque and pitiful scenes must have been at least twenty years in the past, a depressing reminder for a young woman with much of life, she hoped, still before her.

Another problem was Lilian Gifford, who had every intention of making her home with Hardy, whom she called her "daddy-uncle". "The niece has just returned," reported Florence in August, in a letter which shows talents her more studied literary efforts conceal. "I am reminded by her a dozen times a day that 'dear Aunt' was a very great lady and that I am—so she implies—a very low sort of person. Yesterday we had a visit from a bishop's daughter and Miss Gifford said afterwards 'How much she reminded me of dearest Aunt! People connected with the aristocracy of the Church have such perfect manners!' "[29] Carrying the war into the commissariat, Lilian later suggested to Max Gate staff that "the first Mrs. Hardy was a lady and the second was not." From the first, as her letters show, Florence was hypersensitive to these slights on her social origins.

Hardy, though pale and tired, appeared cheerful and had not suffered a serious fit of depression for some time. He seems to have assumed all along that Florence would certainly marry him. As he later wrote simply to Mrs. Henniker, "I am rather surprised that you were surprised ... the course seeming an obvious one to me, being as I was, so lonely and helpless."[30] The idea that it might be surprising for *Florence* to marry a publicly-grieving widower, forty years older than herself, had apparently not occurred to him. The ironic reversal of roles was now complete. Emma, by dying, had become the unattainable beloved. Florence, who for so many years had played this part, was now to be re-cast as everyday companion and helper. "He wanted a housekeeper who could be a companion and read to him—etc.—so I came in," was her rather bleak summing up of her new role.[31] Hardy's parlour-maid, Nellie Titterington, later summed up the situation with a mature and sympathetic judgment many professional scholars might envy. "Myself, I do not think he thought of them as women, but just shadowy figures, fitting into a space like a jigsaw."[32]

The question remains: why did Florence agree to marry Hardy on these unromantic terms? Thanks to the Stoker legacy she was comparatively independent: she even considered "a little London flat to write without interruption". She was not in love with him, as the tone of her letters to Clodd shows, and had for years been in love with another man, now dead. Money played no part in her decision, for she was so unaware of Hardy's solid fortune that at one time she believed he might need a civil list pension.[33] Fame, perhaps, influenced her, and, it must be admitted, Hardy's social connections, his carefully-casual references to titled ladies by their pet names.[34]

She wanted these connections not only for herself, but to launch her younger sisters, for whom she dreamt of "good" marriages.[35] Perhaps she felt, like many women, that three meals a day and clean shirts could be more interestingly supplied to a man of letters than to a man of business, though this illusion cannot long have survived the housekeeping at Max Gate. More than anything, it seems likely that Hardy's obvious need moved her, his loneliness, his helplessness, his reliance on her for all the problems of everyday life. She

had cared for a series of invalids, the elderly, the confused, the be-
reaved: her mother, the tubercular Alfred Hyatt, mad Lady Stoker,
sad Sir Thornley, muddled Emma and grieving Florence Henniker.
"I am never so happy," she once said in a moment of self-revelation,
"as when I have someone to take care of."[36] Life was to take her
at her word.

The final decision was forced by Lilian Gifford, who came to spend
Christmas 1913 at Max Gate. "My niece and Miss Dugdale are here,
ministering to my wants. I don't know what I should do without
them," wrote Hardy to Mrs. Henniker,[37] apparently quite unaware
of the bitter resentment between the two women. Florence had a
bad cold, but refused to stay in bed and leave the field to Lilian;
her nerves were at snapping point. She poured out her troubles to
kind Henry, Mary and Kate, who had no love for the Gifford family.
She said she could not go on at Max Gate "under the conditions
of the past twelve months, but must have some position of authority". All agreed the ménage-à-trois was impossible. Armed with
this support, Florence presented her ultimatum. "If the niece is to
remain here as one of the family," she told Clodd, "then I will not
enter into that compact of which I spoke to you last summer. This
must be decided in a week and if it is settled that she stays, I return
to my own home and stay there." Faced with the threat of revolution,
Hardy at once capitulated. Lilian was sent home. Florence and
Hardy celebrated the last day of 1913 with a visit to Emma's grave.
Kate Hardy, who saw them at Stinsford churchyard, remarked
cheerfully that she "never saw two such dismal 'critters' in her
life".[38] Already the pattern of the future was being laid down.

It was now a year since Emma Hardy's death and two years since
Alfred Hyatt's. Plans for the wedding of the two survivors went forward in strict secrecy. Hardy ruled that, "on account of the press
people", not even relatives were to be told.[39] This was hard for the
large and affectionate Dugdale and Taylor families, but Florence's
parents respected his wishes. Florence rather timidly asked for a
settlement on her marriage, "but it seemed to annoy my husband,
so I desisted".[40] She may have received an engagement ring and wedding gift, but neither is recorded. She and Hardy had already bought
a rough-haired terrier puppy born in August 1913. She felt Max Gate
was so isolated that it needed "a dog that would bark"; in fact they
had improved on this by providing a dog that would bite, the
dreaded Wessex. This, too, would be part of the pattern.

On 29 January 1914, Hardy wrote to Florence at her parents'
house. He visited her there, and was observed by curious Enfield
residents, sharing the family pew at St. Andrew's Church.[41] The
Enfield Gazette reported that Mr. and Mrs. Dugdale had "long been
members of Mr. Hardy's select circle", while Miss Florence Dugdale

had been his assistant "for the past ten years or so". Hardy was later to write telling various friends how long and affectionately Florence had known Emma, adding to Mrs. Henniker that a second marriage "need not obliterate an old affection".[42] Florence, having rebelled at a physical ménage-à-trois, found herself forced to accept a ghostly one.

The carefully concealed wedding was at eight o'clock on a Tuesday morning, 10 February 1914. The little party walked quietly to the parish church. It was a fine morning and the doors stood open, but at that early hour not a soul looked in. By twenty-past eight the service was over and they walked home to 5 River Front, Thomas and Florence Hardy in front with twenty-year-old Marjorie beside them, Henry Hardy and Mr. Dugdale following behind. Not another soul had been present, not even Hardy's sisters or Florence's mother.[43] Florence, in keeping with the subdued ceremony, wore a dark travelling costume and heavy felt hat; "there never was a more unbridal dress and hat than mine, both atrociously ugly".[44] There was a quiet breakfast before Mr. Dugdale hurried back to school at 10.45 a.m.; it would take more than a world-famous son-in-law to deflect the headmaster of St. Andrew's School from his appointed duty. In any case he mistrusted the "indulgent parents and unruly boys" of the twentieth century, feeling "discipline has to be kept up by some amount of severity on my part".[45] Hardy congratulated himself that they had escaped reporters; "we were well out of it". There was no need for Florence to change before they crossed the road to Enfield Town Station. Through these streets she had walked as a romantic, ambitious schoolgirl. Now she was leaving them as the wife of England's greatest author; but it was a sober occasion.

Part II
Florence Hardy

9

"If My Name Were Gifford"

So Florence returned to Max Gate for the first time as a wife. The damp, ugly house still daunted her, but she determined to change its atmosphere. Almost her first action was to write to Edward Clodd, inviting him to stay. He had done more than anyone else to help them in the past five unmarried years. All the same, she felt apologetic, "as your week-ends at Aldeburgh are so very bright and cheerful". She and Hardy, she wrote, "have settled down & become a very humdrum married couple".[1] Was this a hint that the Aldeburgh days were no longer to be mentioned? When he came on 27 February, she was delighted that "our dear & kind Mr. Clodd should be our first guest". It set the seal on "this new estate",[2] and the part she now hoped to play. To Sydney Cockerell she wrote, "I married ... to express my devotion." This was to be the key-note.

All the same, and in spite of the approval of most of Hardy's oldest and most distinguished women friends, Lady Jeune, Lady Ilchester, and Alda, Lady Hoare, there were pitfalls in the way of being herself a distinguished hostess. One was the tiny spare bedroom. The rolling, nautical figure of Clodd made it seem as cramped as a ship's cabin. His *Lotus* would have been larger. She persuaded Hardy, in the first euphoria of marriage, to agree to extend a bay, and throw open a window to the west. She saw a day when "we may have two or three people together to amuse one another". With the builders in, she and Hardy left for Cambridge. It was her first public appearance as his wife, and she revelled in it, the distinguished company of scholars and literati. In London it was the same, among the titled ladies and statesmen. Nor was she too subserviently overawed, at least in private. At Lady Jeune's, in June, "Mr. and Mrs. Winston Churchill came to dinner—but!"

Yet there was still the shadow of Emma, however tactfully people kept off the subject. Even after remarriage, Hardy was obsessed. In May he took Florence to Plymouth, "a rather depressing quest—to find the grave of the late Mrs. Hardy's parents".[3] The hospitable Quiller-Couch, whom they had met in Cambridge, invited them to his house at Fowey in Cornwall, on a yachting estuary reminiscent of Clodd's at Aldeburgh. To the embarrassment of Lady Quiller-Couch and her daughter, Hardy insisted on praising his former wife, and speaking about his courtship of Emma in Cornwall, in spite of

10   Florence with "Wessex" at Max Gate soon after her marriage

the fact that the newly-married Florence was sitting with them.[4]
What Q, a model of courtesy, thought is not recorded, though he
maintained to the end of his life that Hardy's vision of Emma had
been sheer fantasy. There was yet another silent reminder of Emma
at Max Gate which weighed on Florence. Emma had been a frugal
housewife and a good manager. Hardy was used to giving her the
bare minimum for housekeeping. Florence was soon at sea with this.

She had to raid her own dress-allowance, "which makes me feel very disagreeable", she confessed. Although thirty-five years old, she had remained a daughter-at-home, with little experience of domestic responsibility. "I think your housekeeping almost miraculous," she wrote helplessly after a visit to Lady Hoare at Stourhead. "Beside it my own is very poor. But I comfort myself by reflecting that a very small household is more expensive in proportion." A week later she enclosed her accounts for the month of June 1914. "I try to make £20 cover everything—food—servants' wages—cleaning materials—lighting (oil, candles)—postage of parcels etc."[5] The Hoares responded to this cry for help with timely gifts of game in the shooting season. Staff, with three servants, proved no easier than bills. With her usual lack of domestic judgment, and with perhaps over-hasty sympathy, she engaged a deaf-and-dumb girl, the parlour-maid's sister, to help in the house. The experiment failed, and proved "a great nuisance". Above all, Florence had inherited Emma's cook, Jane Riggs, who privately decided that the second Mrs. Hardy "was not a lady" like the first.

In August 1914 the outbreak of war swept aside household considerations. Florence, unthinkingly romantic, was thrilled at the idea of young men going to sacrifice, but had harsh words for the more realistic working-people, who were slow to volunteer, and had no zest for what she called "doing nobly". She found a sympathetic correspondent in Alda, Lady Hoare, whose son, the heir to Stourhead, had at once joined up. Pages were filled with well-meaning but somewhat high-flown sentiments. Florence had adopted the upper-class views which sent a whole generation into meaningless holocaust. In November she saw in London *The Dynasts*, shortened and adapted by Granville-Barker as "a patriotic drama". She was deeply moved when, with the rest of the audience, she joined Henry Ainley speaking in unison "God Save the King". Hardy had no such gestures to offer. He was horribly afraid of German invasion, and would not go to stay with Clodd any more on the dangerous East Coast. He grudged Florence's absence for a single day. He would not venture to London. Her dreams of moving in London society, still more of making Max Gate a social centre, vanished almost overnight.

There was another dream which was shattered too this December. Hardy's new book of poems, *Satires of Circumstance*, pained her "horribly ... I read it with horrible fascination". No wonder: for the few, gentle tributes to herself were drowned in the passionate reminiscences of his wooing of Emma, released on the flood-tide of her death and his remorseful guilt. Florence was stunned. "It seems that I am an utter failure."[6] It seemed too that he no longer loved her. "We are not at all happy," she wrote to Clodd, rapturous in his own second marriage.[7] She began to unbridle her tongue, secretly, about Emma and the Giffords generally. Hardy had invited Lilian for Christmas, and "I expect she will be very rude to me". The New Year and the chilly house brought Florence a severe attack of sciatica, about which Hardy seemed indifferent, though she begged him to take her to Bath for a cure. The summer was worse, for her usual nose and throat trouble persisted so much that a minor operation was advised. In the last week in May 1915 she went into a London nursing-home, where a specialist, Macleod Yearsley, operated on her nose. Relying on her legacy from Sir Thornley, Hardy made no suggestion of paying for all this, though, as she later wrote, "if my name were Gifford" a cheque would have been at once forthcoming. The only compensation was a convalescent stay with Lady Jeune, who managed to cheer her with an ironic piece of gossip about Emma and her relations. When she got home, she also enjoyed Hardy's open discomfiture at Emma's nephew, Gordon, marrying the daughter of a station-master. "What would the Archdeacon say?" commented Florence acidly.

Florence's position, after only just over a year of marriage, was barely tenable. Particularly galling was the restraint placed by Hardy on her generous impulses. "My instinct would be to make this a second home for the people I liked"; yet Hardy—and here she was for the first time in her life openly critical—seemed quite without any sense of social obligation to anyone. Morbidly sensitive as usual, she felt people would blame her for his inhospitality, though she managed to break down resistance to visitors in one or two special instances. Her sister Margaret came to stay in July, Constance Dugdale in August and Clodd with his own newly-married young second wife in September.[8]

Such summer visits reassured her that Hardy was not really a "recluse" as she had feared. Yet, if she had read the signs, any unwonted social liveliness by Hardy might hold dangers for her happiness in another way. She might have remembered that when they themselves first met, her own youth and beauty had caused a startling revival of his interest in life. She might have suspected—perhaps did suspect—a new young feminine interest for the perpetually susceptible poet. Luckily, the provider of this interest was not only sensible but happily married. Mr. Hanbury, the middle-aged squire of the local big house, Kingston Maurward, had installed a young wife there, a niece by marriage of Lady Jeune. The house itself held associations of early love for the seventy-five-year-old Hardy, always apt to confuse a romantic setting with a romantic attachment, as he had done with Emma in Cornwall. He hung wistfully about the great house which, Florence noted, was the only one in the neighbourhood he cared to visit.[9] How much she also noted his attraction to this "*very* good-looking girl" is unknown. Did she know he gave her a signed portrait and a copy of *Under the Greenwood Tree*, also signed? What she may well not have known is that a short and pathetic poem about the house, *In Her Precincts*, actually spoke of his vague longings over the young wife. She may well have thought that it referred to his actual adolescence, not to his endlessly adolescent old age. Mrs. Hanbury ended as a close friend of Florence, and Hardy managed to convert inspiration into a later poem not about her but about her baby daughter, to whom he stood godfather.

So the incident ended happily; but it remained a portent for Florence's future, which she might have been wise to have observed more closely. She had much to absorb her this summer and autumn in the way of personal and family matters. There was, first, the deeply personal question of an "heir" for Max Gate and the Hardy property, which included a house in High West Street, Dorchester, and another in Puddletown. When they had married in 1914, she believed Hardy "would have welcomed a child". Whether this was, at any time, a physical possibility, is another matter, and a remark by Florence to an intimate woman friend seems to indicate that it was probably not. Certainly, within eighteen months, Florence had accepted the fact that "we Hardys, alas, have no bright young faces to take the places of those who go".[10] Equally certainly, by summer 1915, Florence was urging the claims of a relative of Hardy who was about her own age, "the only decent relation" in her opinion. This was a distant cousin, Frank George, who had recently qualified as a barrister. Unluckily for Florence's plans, he joined up and was instantly killed in Gallipoli. A few months later there was another family tragedy. Hardy's beloved sister Mary died. Florence had loved the simple, responsible, reticent woman, who had accepted her at once into the family circle; but she was horrified by the squabbling of the other Hardys over Mary's small inheritance. Her second big disillusion in the first two years of marriage was the sordidness of real village life, in contrast with the idyllic pictures she had painted of it at Enfield, and in print. The first disillusion was, of course, the shock of what it was really like to live with a famous author. She could still write, on the second anniversary of marriage, "on the whole—in spite of my profuse grumbling—I think no two years could have been happier".[11] Yet before the same letter was finished, the "grumbling" had broken out again. Florence, nurtured on dreams, was finding reality increasingly distasteful.

Indeed, the beginning of a third year plunged her inexperience into very deep waters. To her horror, news reached Max Gate, early in 1916, that Edward Clodd was planning to publish his reminiscences. Would they contain references to her many premarital stays at Aldeburgh as "the Lady" of Thomas Hardy? Instead of trusting to Clodd's kindly discretion, she took panic action. Angrily and fatally impulsive, she sent the always-friendly Clodd a stinging and threatening letter. If he mentioned her and Hardy, she would get her husband to "write to the papers about it". What she meant, or how much her panic was prompted by Hardy himself, will probably never be known; but it was an error of judgment fatal to friendship. When Clodd's *Memories* came out later that year, and proved innocuous, she sought to retrieve her mistake by attempting to write to him on the old footing; but things were never the same. It was the first and one of the worst of many such lapses. Her limited upbringing and experience were often inadequate to stand the test of the sophisticated world, into which she had so ambitiously won a precarious way from Enfield.

Enfield indeed was where her truest and most reliable feelings were still centred; to her family there she could still be her natural, straightforward and loving self, released from an element of falsity, in which she was always dangerously out of her depth. Early in the New Year there was disquieting news from the Dugdale home. Florence's strong, self-reliant father, still active as he approached retirement—he was now sixty-three—suddenly went down with a mysterious illness. In his school log-book he recorded this as "muscular rheumatism", causing him lameness and intense pain, which several times compelled him to miss school. Florence, however, as soon as she could leave Hardy (also ill), visited Enfield, and found him, she wrote,[12] "dangerously ill ... a deplorable wreck", suffering from "a complete nervous breakdown". Against her alarmist diagnosis, it must be recorded that the doctor confirmed Mr. Dugdale's own description of his illness, and that her father, after a long holiday that year with his wife's Brighton relatives, continued to teach beyond retirement age until 1919, and live, apparently hale and hearty, to be eighty-four.[13] Indeed, Florence's nervous apprehension was to find family woe and grief everywhere. Her mother, always an invalid, seemed particularly unwell, and unable to find a servant, since all the local girls were going into the armaments factory. War brought other family worries. Her youngest sister Marjorie had become engaged to a young man in the Royal Flying Corps. Then Eva Dugdale, nursing wounded soldiers in Brighton, had difficulties, in spite of Florence's efforts to help her. It was a catalogue of domestic disaster, which a quick summer visit to Brighton, to see aunts, father, mother, and Eva did nothing to allay. Florence, always neurotically fearing the worst, became a prophetess of doom, though at her sister's wedding in 1917, to which she took the cheerful Kate Hardy, she conceded that Marjorie looked charming in a white velour hat with the badge of the RFC worked on it in gold. In spite of Hardy's grumbles, she had the young couple to honeymoon at

Max Gate.[14] 1917, too, brought another sister, Connie, into the circle
of Florence's worries. She, according to Florence, had an uncon-
scious grievance against Florence, Ethel, and now Marjorie, because
they had married.

Though sometimes flying to unwarranted extremes, all these
anxieties show where Florence's best loves and most enduring affec-
tions lay—with her family. Such concerns were still the real stuff
of Florence's life. They even took precedence over her feelings for
her husband, and coloured some of her attitude toward him. She
contrasted bitterly his behaviour toward her family with his behaviour toward his late wife and her relations. When she spoke of going
to Brighton again, and suggested even that he should take her, as
she knew from diaries he had taken Emma, he objected, and she
commented, "If some of the Gifford family lived there, of course
he would be very eager to go."[15] Resentfully, she told a friend she
herself would not spend her life entertaining Gifford relatives at Max
Gate, and she announced (inaccurately, as it proved) that Emma's
nephew Gordon, who had been practically brought up by the
Hardys, would never again be invited. The shadow of Emma pervaded the house, and even the garden. "I may not alter the shape
of a garden bed"—though she won from Hardy the concession of
an asparagus bed, provided she paid for it.

Such things made her vision of sharing a great writer's life a mockery. She had already decided "deep within me, that my husband
rather dislikes my being a scribbling woman".[16] The chief blow was
his rejection of what she had hoped was her proudest boast, to be
his prime literary inspiration. The dead Emma had totally fore-
stalled her. She concluded the disastrous year of 1916 with the most
cynical possible summary of the life she had chosen for herself in
marriage.[17]

> My husband is very well & amazingly cheerful in spite of his gloomy
> poems. I wish people knew that he was really happy, for strangers
> must imagine that his only wish is to die & be in the grave with the
> only woman who ever gave him any happiness.

Announcing that in January 1917 she would be thirty-six, when in
fact she would be thirty-eight, she was not only beginning the familiar process of trying to defeat time by reducing her admission of
age. She was beginning to feel desperately old, and, in the repressive
atmosphere, almost as old as Hardy. "Sometimes I feel *eighty*," she
concluded, after barely three years of marriage. Fortunately, there
were comparatively better things to come in the New Year of 1917,
though even these were to have for Florence their curious and
characteristic humiliations.

10

"A Tremendous Job in Hand"

IN SPITE OF what were now the unpromising circumstances of her life, Florence had never given up the dream of writing. However correct she was to feel that her husband disliked "a scribbling woman", unless as amanuensis, or typist-helper of his own tasks, she determined to prise out time to insert some attempt at her own "literary" work into the welter of housekeeping, routine letter-writing, and secretarial chores. Even if it could only be, as it were, carried on the back of some greater talent than she could ever possess, publication was for her the one most desired goal.

One obvious means was to capitalize the minor but undoubted genius of the artist E. J. Detmold, for whose children's picture-books, in 1911 and 1912, Florence had provided her natural history "descriptions". Hodder had evidently found these good sellers, and they had already approached Florence with the idea that she might provide the text for a similar set of pictures of dogs. In the first year of married life, she felt her duty lay with Hardy; but in 1915, when he proved so plainly that his consideration for her as a person had waned, she felt that an act of literary self-assertion had to be made, if only to restore her confidence. The publisher's idea had expanded from dogs merely to domestic pets generally. This had appealed to the quirky strain in Detmold, and suited the minute, odd, concentrated intensity of his miniaturist talent. Hence Florence found herself writing not only about conventional pets, dogs, cats, rabbits, guinea-pigs, but attempting to embellish the lives of lizards, tree-frogs, tortoises, and goldfish.

Her text certainly manages to show great empathy with animals of all sorts, even the unusual ones. Mainly designed to teach children to take a kindly, intelligent care of their pets, it abounds in helpful warnings. "Should a strange Goldfish be put with others they will often hunt it to death." It also conveys, though coyly expressed, the message that nursing mothers need special attention.

> While Mrs. Bunny is feeding her young, she should have, for herself, a good supply of green food, and now and then a warm mash of milk and barley meal.

Prose descriptions of this sort are not only practical, but fairly successful in style. On the other hand, as always, Florence's ventures into verse are a disaster, as in the case of this unfortunate bird.

> The "cordon bleu", as you may have heard,
> Is a fanciful name for a dicky bird,
> Who is really a finch. However, the word
> Refers to our breast colours, it is averred.

"Cordon bleu", far from being "a fanciful name for dicky bird", is the most generally-accepted dealer's name for the African finch. Florence's verse is an embarrassment to this plain fact. Even more embarrassing in tone is what she produces for "Love Bird".

> If you have not seen us, at sometime you will,
> Perched close up together with bill against bill;
> And on hearing our quaint little noises like kisses,
> You'll say, "There are few prettier pictures than this is!"

Such verses make it all the more obvious when Hardy, as with her two previous Detmold books, was persuaded to provide anonymously some verse of his own. The manuscript of "The Lizard" was later acknowledged by Florence as his, and, after sixty years in limbo, now appears in his *Complete Poems*. Unacknowledged, but characteristic of Hardy, is "Tortoises".

> Rather insensible people are we
> On the tops of our shells, or are thought so to be
> By many who speak concerning it,
> Including among them a certain wit,
> Who, when a little girl stroked one of us
> And said, "'Tis to please it", replied to her thus,
> As smart on the shoulder he tapped her,
> "Caresses are vain on those hard, shelly walls.
> You might as well stroke, dear, the dome of St. Paul's,
> To please the Dean and Chapter."

The ending, at least, seems to be Hardy, an able practitioner of light verse, anticipating in technique, and in a certain style of sardonic humour, his later, adult satire beginning

> Said the grave Dean of Westminster:
> Mine is the best minster . . .

A Book of Baby Pets was published in March 1915. During this year and the next, Florence found herself increasingly alone, with Hardy upstairs in the study writing poem after poem, not one, as she reflected bitterly, in any way touching their past love. He seemed to have renounced past friendships too, and become, by June 1915, "a recluse". By New Year 1916, she complained, he "stays in his study . . . and does not come downstairs at all", even when his own brother and sister called. But for the dog Wessex, Florence would have been alone for "literally thousands" of evenings. Nor would he invite anyone to the house, even for a meal. Florence felt miserably that old friends, to whom Hardy and she owed gratitude and hospitality, such as Dora and Clement Shorter, would blame her.

At the end of 1915, with Hardy driven even deeper into himself by Mary's death, she re-established contact with Shorter. The result was an engagement by the generous editor of *The Sphere* for her to review new novels on a freelance basis. It was not very distinguished work, but the next year found Florence managing to fit these brief efforts in among her domestic duties, in spite of "lots of work"—that is, typing letters—for Hardy. This was not without strain, in an uncomfortable house with its primitive equipment and no bathroom, only a hip bath containing barely three pints of water—"and I love a really nice hot bath", lamented Florence. She felt "severely run down", and Macleod Yearsley, her ear, nose and throat specialist, advised a three weeks' holiday, "but that is impossible". The only form of "holiday" Hardy would recognize was an expedition with him to Emma's haunts in Cornwall, and that was all, in 1916, that Florence got.[1]

Still, she had some comfort from her reviewing, a life-line to her literary dreams, even though she felt her "journalistic spirit" distressed her husband, and herself admitted that she had some "awful trash" to review. At first she did not even write reviews herself, but vetted novels for Shorter to include in his own "Literary Letter". *The Sphere* received at least half-a-dozen novels a week, of which Shorter himself could only read the one recommended by Florence. However, early in 1916, a feature called "Some New Books of the Hour" was started to deal with the back-log of novels. Florence wrote this, though her "reviews" are mainly plot-summaries, and any opinions are cautiously and conventionally expressed. The main type of book with which she was entrusted was, as she said, "trash". Shorter still bagged the best books, or gave them to Clodd, who signed his own reviews. Florence remained, as usual, anonymously in the background. There are hardly any individual sparks, except over one novel, *The Honest Lawyer*, set in Dorchester and Wareham, which she suspected, typically, of using local people, living or dead, as copy.

However, the chief stumbling-block to Florence's reviewing, which contributed more than anything else to her giving it up at the end of 1916, was Hardy's attitude to Shorter. In mid-March he showed resentment at a parcel of books from the editor to Florence, which Hardy had to acknowledge as Florence had hurried off to her sick father at Enfield. Hardy's letter was irritated, not to say downright rude. Not that he was without some reason for annoyance. Shorter, like many self-educated bibliophiles, of whom the most notorious was the forger T. J. Wise, produced a series of privately-printed pamphlets, which he entitled "A Bookman's

Hobby''. These had included reprints of several poems by Hardy, after magazine publication but before Hardy could collect them in book-form. He pestered Hardy for such permissions, and Hardy was getting restive to the point of open sarcasm.[2] "I don't care", he wrote, "to have them printed in your pet limited edition. Of course, if what you say is true—that anybody may print such an edition of anybody's writings without permission, you must do your worst."[3] When in April 1916, Hardy's poem *To Shakespeare After Three Hundred Years*, a favourite of Florence's, was requested by Shorter for his reprints, he met with downright refusal and rebuke. "I cannot very well agree to a reprint of the Shakespeare poem. Apart from that, I fancy you are getting off the track with these private printings." The fact was, Hardy and his own pet bibliophile, Sydney Cockerell, had concocted a plan which involved Florence's passive co-operation. Henceforward, any such special limited editions would be produced "as printed for Florence Emily Hardy", under her nominal editorship, though really under the supervision of Cockerell. Once more, Florence found herself being used as a convenient means, a pawn in the literature game instead of, as she always hoped, a queen. Shorter had been genuinely kind to her, even if such kindness may have been mixed with self-interest in pushing his own editions. She was now put in the position of repaying that kindness by producing something which looked like a deliberate snub to the editor. Shorter's friendly references to both the Hardys in his "Literary Letter" grew noticeably less in the second half of 1916.

Florence's consequent frustrations took toll of her health in 1917. She was all too ready to listen to doctors, and had a series of expensive inoculations. She was also all too ready to lash out at Emma's relatives. "If I were a Gifford of course all this would be paid for me ... Were I Lilian Gifford, the cheque would be written immediately." Her illnesses were partly signs of her repression. However, in 1917, Florence's secretarial duties for Hardy brought on quite real eyestrain, since he now hardly wrote a letter himself. She was becoming primarily a secretary (unpaid) rather than a wife. By September 1917, though failing to find assistance for secretarial work, she had adopted "a tremendous pair of horn spectacles", which helped her to carry on. This was as well since, as she also mysteriously announced to a friend at that time, "I have a tremendous job in hand—literary".[4] This fresh and unnamed employment was, in some ways, to rule her life for the next ten years.

It arose partly from the fright she and Hardy had experienced, in the previous year, from Clodd's projected reminiscences. How was one to insure that the world received only an impression of Hardy's (and her) life which was acceptable to Florence and himself? She could hardly write letters forbidding all old friends to mention them, nor hope for kindly acquiescence, such as Clodd had eventually shown. Should she therefore herself write Hardy's authorized biography, to forestall others? Yet this at once posed difficulties. Hardy had been in his mid-sixties when she first met him. Even Boswell had to reconstruct only the first fifty-four years of Dr. Johnson's life. Nor perhaps did Hardy trust her unaided efforts. After all, her only two serious, published literary efforts, the two stories in the *Cornhill*, had been written, virtually or entirely, by him; so, even on a smaller scale, had the only verses showing any competence in the three Detmold books. Hardy had to face the fact that his self-styled "scribbling woman" had very little natural, individual talent.

Yet this realization itself produced the novel solution which came to constitute one of the most remarkable, unspoken deceptions in all English literature. Briefly, Hardy constructed for Florence a scheme by which he himself wrote his autobiography, in the third person throughout, so that it could be published after his death under her name, F. E. Hardy. Once more, her chance of immortality was reduced to lending her name to something written by him. After all, no one had spotted the deception involved in the two *Cornhill* stories. With Hardy's careful public build-up about his second wife's literary talents, the future would accept, indeed did accept, for some time after his death, the fiction that this was not a disguised autobiography, but an objective biography by Florence. "Thus", as Hardy was reported to have once incautiously admitted, was insured what he called "absolute accuracy". In his terms, this meant telling only as much about his life as he (and Florence) wanted known.

One of the aims was, of course, to conceal all their expeditions together before Emma was dead, particularly those which they had taken before she knew of Florence's existence. So *The Life* implies that all their visits to Clodd at Aldeburgh were taken by Hardy alone. Florence's name is never mentioned. When they go off to Ventnor together in March 1910, Florence appears as "a friend" (unnamed). When in 1911 the two holiday in Gloucester, though indeed chaperoned on that occasion by Kate Hardy, the visit is described as arising from Hardy's desire to study the architecture of the cathedral, and it is implied that he "made a journey" for that purpose quite unaccompanied. Thus Florence, from the first, was required to be the apparent author of a work in which she entirely wrote herself out of Hardy's life until her wedding-day when, in Hardy's laconic third-person phrase, "the subject of this memoir married the present writer".

In fact, once again, Florence's hoped-for "literary" job turned out to be humiliatingly secretarial. Her task was to arrange in chronological order all Hardy's old letters and notebooks. He then selected from them, himself writing the results up in third person narration,

11   Hardy and Florence in their garden, about 1920

destroying most of the originals as he went. The result was then
typed by Florence, after which his own tell-tale manuscript was
similarly consigned to the flames. Any alterations in the typescript
were made by him, and less frequently by her, in a deliberate typo-
graphical hand, to keep up the pretence. Not even in conversation
or letters to intimates did Florence reveal this process. She even kept

up the deception with the publishers, who were eventually to print the result over her name. In January 1925, just three years before Hardy's death, she wrote to Sir Frederick Macmillan, with apparently studied casualness:[5]

> You may remember I once wrote to you of a quantity of notes I had accumulated from time to time of Mr. Hardy's conversations, memoranda etc., which he says I can use if any biography of him should be wanted.

The last three years of Hardy's life were particularly exacting for Florence. If the "biography" were really only "a quantity of notes" three years before his death, it could hardly have taken shape by the time he died. Yet only ten months after his death, the first volume of Florence's so-called biography appeared in print. It is impossible that it could have been written, revised, proof-read, printed in such a short time. It must have been virtually completed many years before. In fact, as the typescript shows, all Florence had time to do, in these months after Hardy's death, was to remove nearly every complimentary remark that Hardy had written about Emma. Her sole original work was the negative one of eliminating signs of her husband's adulation of her past rival, by crossing out passages referring to Emma's energy, dash, social successes, and kindnesses. Neither it, nor its sequel in 1930, *The Later Years of Thomas Hardy*, are any more the work of F. E. Hardy than the two *Cornhill* stories were the work of F. E. Dugdale. Even its Prefatory Note, signed by the initials F. E. H., bears every mark of Hardy's hand in its phrasing, style, and attitude.

Whatever may be thought of this work, whether as a literary curiosity, or, more censoriously, as a confidence trick upon its readers, there is no doubt of its eventual effect upon Florence. It killed, at long last, her pathetic ambitions to write on her own account, the author she had tried from girlhood to be. Her letters to intimate friends reveal this all too clearly. In 1917, fanned by a sympathetic new friendship, the flame was still burning. "I want to plunge anew into a literary career."[6] Three solid years of playing second fiddle to her husband, and knowing her own words were accounted of little value beside his, changed once and for all her ardent, hopeful if misguided ambition. "All literary work of my own is put a stop to," she wrote,[7] almost exactly three years later, on 25 May 1920. "However, what I should have done would probably have been valueless, and so it may be as well that it was never done." The dream of writing, which had ruled half her life, for at least the past twenty years, was over. At forty, she must find other consolations if she could. Could she, without actually writing, perhaps make some mark in the literary world as the hostess of Max Gate?

11

"Regarded and Treated as Hostess"

THE CHIEF DIFFICULTY in accepting Hardy's autobiography as Florence's composition is, of course, that it is written in an idiom totally unlike that of Florence's own generation. It is not the writing of a fairly young woman but of an old man, whose allusions, references, jokes even, are of an age long before hers. After all, Hardy was born over a decade before her own father. When Florence had been only six years old, Hardy had submitted to George du Maurier, the *Punch* artist, a suggestion for a joke in that periodical.[1] The humour is so feeble, and, above all, so old-fashioned even for its own time, that it is clear Hardy's normal idiom was more like the style Florence's grandparents might have used. Yet it was this style, dutifully copied on Florence's typewriter, that the world was going to be asked to accept, after Hardy's death, as Florence's natural utterance.

Quite apart from its effect on the credibility of her authorship, this was a parallel situation to her life since her marriage with Hardy—that is, for the past three years. For company, companionship, and correspondence, she had inherited, through him, people of his own generation, far older than hers. Her first Max Gate guest had been Edward Clodd, born in exactly the same year as Hardy. Her main local friend, Mary Sheridan of Frampton, the lively daughter of the distinguished American historian Motley, was also born in the 1840s, and Hardy had known her over thirty years. Other women friends, such as Lady Jeune, were, if not as old as her husband, those she got to know through him, and at least twenty years older than herself. Her two chief women correspondents were Rebekah Owen and Alda, Lady Hoare, with both of whom she exchanged a large series of letters during the first three years of marrriage. For long periods, she averaged one letter a week to each of them.

Both ladies were older than Florence and, though unlike in most respects, had one quality in common which made them desirable outlets for her correspondence. Both had known Emma Hardy, and had formed unfavourable opinions of Hardy's first marriage. Though Lady Hoare was too well-bred and discreet to reveal this in so many words, she had been the recipient herself of some of Emma's diatribes over Hardy, her complaints that he was "not as

formerly", and had doubtless had her own opinions of a wife who
could protest in such an uncontrolled way. As for Miss Owen, who
had known Emma for the last twenty years of her life, she had
formed an unfavourable, not to say prejudiced impression, and
expressed it freely and frequently. She never forgot that, on her con-
version to Catholicism, the Evangelical Emma had roundly condemned her new beliefs. Both ladies were out-and-out worshippers
of Hardy himself and all his works, though one was the wife of an
English landowner of 6,000 acres, and the other, Miss Owen, a
wealthy American settled in the Lake District. For Florence, the
common factor in their very differing natures was that both would
receive sympathetically her pent-up feelings about Emma and the
Giffords.

Florence, in fact, was adept at catching the tone of a correspondent. To Miss Owen, more frank and American, her dislike of
Hardy's displays of feeling about Emma were strongly, even
crudely, expressed. Hardy's pilgrimages to Plymouth, Emma's
birthplace, were tartly dismissed as being taken "to gaze, once again,
I suppose, at the house where SHE was born";[2] she sarcastically
quoted Milton to dismiss Emma as Hardy's "late espoused saint".[3]
To Miss Owen she could let herself go about the whole Gifford family,
and Hardy's desire to go and "hunt up Giffords". She pounced on
the Gifford pretensions to gentility, specially those of Emma's niece
Lilian. "My own sisters", she exclaimed, "have to earn their own
living. I don't know why other girls cannot. Of course Lilian and
her people will always have to be kept." She listed bitterly, though
not always accurately, the failings of Emma's dead father and
Emma's nephew, Gordon Gifford.

To Lady Hoare her tone of voice was totally different, though even
here, her dislike and distrust of Lilian Gifford break out. "I am
devoutly hoping and almost *praying*—that she won't carry on her
old mischief-making tactics ... I could not stand that."[4] Hardy's
pilgrimages to the shrines of his former wooing of Emma were
treated in a more oblique way, indeed almost impersonally. "One
has to go through a sort of mental hoodwinking and blind one's self
to the past."[5] To both correspondents Florence, sensing a sympathetic audience, wrote in terms of appreciation which seem so exag-
gerated that one cannot help suspecting their sincerity. It is unlikely
that the letters of both Miss Owen and Lady Hoare, whose wit, style,
and wisdom Florence praises to the skies, can possibly have been
so remarkable or even worthy of publication as Florence suggests.
Nor can both ladies have been such angels of light as Florence makes
out. Lady Hoare, in particular, is "a vision of beautiful, queenly
womanhood", whose judgment in literature is unerring, and whose
skill, even in such mundane matters as housekeeping, is "almost

miraculous". At times, the superlatives become nearly comic. "There is a broad band of radiance falling across our path—and that is *you*!" Partly, this is due to what Florence still believed must constitute "fine writing". One remembers Edward Clodd's relief when the article she wrote for the *Standard* on his birthday appeared in print shorn of the "purple patches" which had so alarmed him.

One feels, though, that it would have been healthier for Florence if, in these first three years of married life, she had had some friend, outside her family, and of her own age, to whom she could unbosom herself, without the sense of obligation she obviously felt to these older ladies. Their virtue in her eyes was that both thought her a better match for Hardy than his first wife had been. They helped to salve the wounds which his obsession with the dead Emma continually caused her. This was not the same as the real friendship between equals that Florence needed, and which, in some ways, she was now happily to find.

In the summer of 1917, she embarked on a fresh course of the expensive inoculations which her sister, Eva the nurse, had said were so useless. They were, however, under the supervision of the ear, nose and throat specialist Macleod Yearsley, who had treated Clodd's young wife, and whose judgment she trusted. Though they probably did her no good physically, they had one great benefit for her psychological well-being. Yearsley had just married the daughter of another medical man, and he took his nervous patient back to tea with his wife. Louisa Yearsley was charming, kind, forthright, and friendly; moreover, she was younger than Florence, quick to imagine what marriage to an old man, in a remote and inconvenient house, must be like. She set herself to draw out the repressed Florence. "I feel I talked volubly & absurdly the whole time," Florence apologized;[7] but she at once warmed to further invitations from her understanding new friend. Louisa took her to the theatre, the cinema—"a new and pleasant experience"—and to the big London shops, Jaeger's, Debenham's, and Heal's, whose modern furniture made her vow to improve matters at Max Gate. Even when condemned to long days and nights back there, she now had a new and sympathetic friend, to whom to write. If she herself had no prospect of a child, as Louisa now had, she could, as it were by proxy, report the progress of Marjorie, who was now also pregnant, though Florence's suggestion that "the event" should take place at Max Gate was hastily scotched by Hardy. Even embroilments with servants could now be shared with the young London housewife. Though Florence's efforts to take cookery lessons alienated Jane Riggs the cook, the last human relic of Emma's regime, she could report to Louisa a domestic success in engaging a new cook, who had, in fact, been a maid-of-all-work in Florence's family home at Enfield.

12   H. G. Wells and Rebecca West visit the Hardys, 1919

Indeed it was as if for Florence youth was breaking into flood again, as the long ice-age of the war began to crack. On the day before armistice, there came a visitor to Max Gate, who proved to be the first of a new, young generation, attracted by the idea of a timeless ancient, whose poetry spoke the new, inspirational language they felt was needed. Hardy's volume, *Moments of Vision*, which had appeared late in 1917, and which contained arguably his finest work, was the magnet which drew them to Max Gate. This first young poet was an attractive, exotic creature, and he charmed not only Hardy but Florence also. Siegfried Sassoon seemed like a visitant from another planet, "one of the most brilliant & likeable young men I know", full of ideas totally new to Florence's world. "Imagine", she wrote of his professed politics, "a son of the Sassoon family & cousin of the Rothschilds, a *Labour* member! ... My head spins."[8] For a woman who had written confidently to Lady Hoare about "a *most* objectionable type of socialist", this was a new generation indeed.

Would it be too much for her, even when introduced and represented by the handsome Sassoon? Although she could not guess his sardonic appraisal of Max Gate, with herself and the glaring portrait of Emma in silent conflict, she must have felt apprehensive about this new young race, all seven to seventeen years her juniors. Within a year, she found herself exposed to one of its keenest brains, in the presence of the new literary woman. New both in ability and in morality, Rebecca West appeared with her own great literary man. Early in 1919, H. G. Wells brought her to Max Gate. The occasion is immortalized in a set of tiny captioned sketches, drawn by Wells, not only a famous novelist but a great comic artist manqué. A Thurber-like figure of Florence, described by Rebecca West herself as "a depressed lady", sits hunched gloomily at tea. Hardy, jauntily naughty, is telling them about the Roman cemetery, on which Max Gate was built. "So I built the house entirely on skelingtons," he announces proudly. "Skelingtons may be healthy but they ain't *gay* soil," comments Florence in dejection, while Rebecca West displays cheerful interest.[9] If the new generation could be wonderfully stimulating, it might also be almost excessively alarming, especially to one whose literary background was as different from it as Florence's had been; yet she found a friend in an older poet, Charlotte Mew.

Perhaps most happily for her, the respect shown to Hardy by other writers generally took the form of deputations, when everyone was on best behaviour, and therefore acting as she felt creative writers should. In 1919, organized by Sassoon, fifty living poets presented him with a volume of holograph poems. In 1920, to mark his eightieth birthday, there was a special delegation from the Society of Authors. In 1921, he received a birthday address from

106 younger writers, together with a first edition of John Keats's 1820 volume. For all the secretarial strain of answering letters and telegrams on such occasions, Florence secretly revelled in these events. An honorary D.Lit. at Oxford was celebrated by a special OUDS production of *The Dynasts*, which Hardy and Florence attended. She was charmed by the old-world chivalry of the undergraduates. When "a wretch" from the Press tried to photograph, he was obliterated by a young man, who flung himself on the camera, exclaiming, "Mr. Hardy is our guest. He shall not be photographed against his will."[10] Unluckily, another pressman had managed to catch Florence in one of her more unfortunate hats, and the picture, "that awful caricature", appeared in the papers, and kept being reproduced, to plague her in after years. Yet, in general, it delighted Florence to be "regarded and treated as hostess", as she afterwards described herself, on such literary and academic occasions.

Individual visitors were more exacting, especially as each summer brought "a vast number of Americans" to Max Gate. They tended, in spite of Florence's admonitions, to write books which mixed appreciation of Hardy's works with domestic details about her household. One of them even dug up for his book the picture of herself at Oxford in the unlucky hat, rousing Florence herself to vituperation:[11] "I disliked the man when I first saw him, and he must have realised this, which accounts for the way in which he writes of me." This visitor, Ernest Brennecke, had, in fact, portrayed the Hardys somewhat satirically—their terrible dog Wessex, Florence's hens, in which, Hardy said, "I am not interested", and Hardy's over-anxious care to give biographers his own self-edited version of his ancestry and upbringing. Young English literary visitors were usually more discreet, and pleased Florence. She found most of them both charming and clever. Reading between the lines, it seems that most of them in turn appreciated her in her difficult role. Special favourites were Walter de la Mare (who actually was a few years older than herself) and Edmund Blunden. The first became virtually her favourite modern poet, the second, she agreed with her husband, had an air of Keats. Life at Max Gate, with Hardy too mellowing in his eighties, was becoming much more as she had once imagined it might be. The handsome Middleton Murry, with his complex private life, was another favourite younger visitor, and Florence stood godmother to one of his children, though toward the end of Hardy's life she confessed to Sassoon, "I never was very fond of Murry."[12] Robert Graves, on the other hand, earned a bad mark by reporting inaccurately conversations at Max Gate. The year 1923 was a bumper occasion with visits from E. M. Forster ("rather fussy about little things"), de la Mare and wife, three calls in the spring from T. E. Lawrence, "a most brilliant magnetic young man", and

even the then Prince of Wales, who had a never-to-be-forgotten
lunch at Max Gate, with a photograph in the garden afterwards on
a hot day in July. Though saddened by the death, in April of that
year, of Mrs. Henniker, Florence's ideal hostess, she could feel that,
as she had always hoped, Max Gate was becoming a social and
literary centre.

The physical amenities of Max Gate, too, were improved to meet
the new social needs. A correspondence with a rich Ohio book-collector provided Florence not only with a supply of delicious American
candies, but the determination to get a proper bathroom, installed
in 1920. She and any guests who stayed the night now had the benefit
of "a glorious big bath and lots of very hot water". Hardy, with
peasant distrust of letting piped water into upper rooms, still compelled the maids to carry up cans for his hip-bath, but for Florence
it was real progress, as was the telephone. A wireless was also introduced, though apparently more for the benefit of the dog Wessex
than for the Hardys. Housekeeping generally was still a nightmare
with "a lack of every labour-saving device"; but at least Florence
had now escaped the terrible loneliness of the war years, the first
four years of marriage. Visitors such as Virginia Woolf might
comment on her nervous manner, but she was at last literally more
at home. She even branched out in 1923 to buy, with her own small
private income, a paddock alongside Max Gate, where she could keep
her chickens, the hens disparaged by Hardy. Members of her own
family came to stay far more frequently, including her much-loved
father, who had at last retired from teaching to a large house in his
wife's home town of Brighton. Her sister Eva, who helped to nurse
Hardy in any crisis of health, also came as a welcome guest, and
enjoyed herself on a summer holiday in 1925. At the same time her
sister Marjorie, who had emigrated to join her husband in Canada,
reappeared with Florence's small nephew, who was, as Florence
wrote, "named Thomas after my husband—whom I hope he may
resemble in as many ways as possible—besides the name".[13]

One can see, in fact, in the first half of the 1920s, a strong vein
of tenderness and affection developing in Florence towards Hardy.
Whether his helplessness touched her, his reliance on her for everything, his occasional alarming illnesses, such as a renewal of his
periodic bladder inflammation in 1922, she began to drop her complaints about his indifference, neglect, and his obsession with his first
wife. Though still an unbeliever, she accompanied Hardy on his
occasional visits to Holy Trinity, Dorchester, though he always
seemed ill at ease, and used to thrust the prayer book at Florence
to find his place, perhaps owing to failing sight.[14] The wonder
expressed by younger pilgrims to Max Gate reinforced her in her
role as Hardy's admiring protector. She watched for signs of tired-

ness or strain, set herself to ward off unwanted intruders, and mar-velled openly that he was producing book after book of poems as his eighties advanced. She did not realize, in her naturally generous instinct, that this new-found tenderness to him might lay her own loving feelings open to some of the worst shocks she had experienced since their strange compact of marriage between youth and age had begun.

12

"Things That One Cannot Write About"

ON 8 AUGUST 1921, Florence wrote to the dramatist and critic St. John Ervine that for the last seven years she had only been away from Max Gate for one clear week, and that spent in a London nursing-home for her operation in 1915. "I begin to feel the strain mentally," she added. Domestically, in spite of the new bathroom, there were still back-breaking difficulties, "e.g. oil lamps (no gas or electric light), all open coal fires ... no main drainage".[1] Florence felt that the house needed at least £500 spending on it. She added, in another letter to the sympathetic Louisa Yearsley, "The strain ... is almost enough to drive one into an asylum."[2]

On the other hand, if nothing else complicated matters, the domestic chores were not insurmountable. Florence had got herself into a routine of work, helped three times a week by the new secretary, Miss O'Rourke, who had joined Max Gate in 1923. She herself still typed Hardy's autobiography, answered more important correspondence, read to him as his eyes weakened, and skirmished in the kitchen with the new cook, now less desirable since she had introduced a husband and a mischievous child. What buoyed Florence up was Hardy's obvious dependence on her, and her feeling that she was the only woman in his life. Yet even this conviction, which made the distasteful aspects of Max Gate seem worthwhile, appeared to Florence, in the first half of the 1920s, to be subtly threatened. Whether or not this new threat was a figment of her advancing forties, it had disastrous results.

Florence, of course, was always at the mercy of attacks of illness, as she had been all her life, mostly centred on ears, nose and throat. Both her local doctor and her London specialist were kept busy with her. X-rays were taken. Discussion of whether one operation or another was necessary filled these years. Florence lived in fear of this; and so, in another way, did Hardy. Since his own illness in 1922, his dependence on her had increased. He felt he could not face her being away for another week in a London nursing-home. In 1923, he is found reasoning in a long letter to Macleod Yearsley against an operation for the removal of a gland from Florence's neck, and saying that "they" (Florence and himself) can put up with the "slight disfigurement" a glandular swelling affords. It is an astonishing letter from the once-loving man, who had implored his old friends

99

to look after the delicate Florence's health. In spite of Hardy's plea,
Yearsley in the next year, 1924, decided an operation was necessary.
Florence had acquired more commitments earlier that year. In
February she took over a post Hardy had recently resigned through
age, and became a Borough Magistrate in Dorchester, a position
which she filled with her usual conscientiousness. There were even
more visitors to entertain, including a sculptor to whom Hardy sat
for a week, and the Balliol Players, who performed one of their Greek
comedies on the lawn at Max Gate. Florence confessed to total
exhaustion, and wrote to Louisa Yearsley of some acute personal
problems—"all sorts of things that one cannot write about". Yearsley, perhaps plotting that a minor operation would at least get
Florence away from Max Gate, admitted her to the Fitzroy House
Nursing Home, Fitzroy Square, on 29 September 1924. The operation, though successful, aged Florence incredibly. In a photograph
taken a month later, she actually looks, as she had once dramatically
said she felt, *"eighty"*, eyes deep-sunken in a worn and tragic face.
Was she, in fact, in the grip of some deep depressive mental state?
Her actions over the next few months certainly lend colour to such
a possibility.

It is true that Hardy had shown her a curious proof of his affection
just at this time. In a strange, moving little poem, he portrayed himself waiting in the darkness at the entrance to Max Gate for a car
to arrive. The car was that in which Florence was travelling back
from London, driven by Hardy's brother Henry and the garage-
hand Voss. Hardy's poem, typically, concentrates on his own
despairing feelings, as other cars pass by, and prove not to be
Florence's. She and her feelings are never mentioned. Yet the verses
are shaken by an emotion—fear, love, loneliness, one does not
know—powerfully connected with Florence. On the other hand, for
the past four or five years a situation had been developing and
threatening, so it appeared to Florence, the whole structure of their
married life.

Florence had always adopted a laughing attitude to Hardy's still-
adolescent worship of young women in their twenties. She had herself been in mid-twenties when he tumbled into love with her, and
she knew the signs. Yet since their marriage she had taken com-
mand, very often by becoming herself a friend of the young woman
involved. Young Mrs. Hanbury, about whom Hardy had written
so wistfully in 1917, had invited Florence in 1920 to go abroad with
her for a few weeks to the Hanburys' beautiful villa on the Italian
Riviera, though, of course, "Alas! it is impossible."[3] At Christmas
1920, there were fresh opportunities for her tactful temporizing. Clement Shorter, her former editor on *The Sphere*, had been shattered
by the unexpected death of his talented Irish wife; but, perhaps tak-

ing example from both Hardy and Clodd, he had reappeared in 1920 with a beautiful, new young bride. A photograph was sent to Max Gate, and Hardy, greatly admiring, forgot his differences with Shorter, and proposed to have the couple to stay. That Christmas, yet another beauty entered the house, in curious and striking circumstances, and at once excited Hardy, who, as one of the maids noticed, "seemed to come out of his shell when talking to younger women as if a light were suddenly breaking through".[4]

Since 1908, a band of local amateur actors, who came to be known as the Hardy Players, had performed fairly regularly, late every year, their own stage-adaptation of a Hardy novel or story in the Corn Exchange, Dorchester. Florence, who had a low opinion of the townspeople generally, "who seem to infect Dorchester", found much about these performances, which she dutifully attended, distasteful. "The times when these hateful plays are being performed are so unsatisfactory."[5] In fact, to judge, perhaps not altogether fairly, from group photographs, some of the local comedy impersonations, in particular, may well have jarred Florence, in contrast with the West End productions she still slipped off to see. However, this Christmas night 1920, she opened Max Gate to the company. They had been performing a version of *The Return of the Native*, and had included in it the scene where Eustacia Vye, dressed as a man, plays the part of the Turkish Knight in the Christmas Mummers. Hardy himself had put together for them a mumming play of St. George, based on versions he had known in boyhood, and on local tradition. As a compliment to him, they came and acted this at his own house, as if they were in fact village mummers. The adolescent Hardy had always been deeply stirred by these village displays; now, among the actors, the eighty-year-old man found an equally moving inspiration. The Eustacia Vye of the play and mumming scene was the beautiful dark-haired daughter of a Dorchester confectioner, Gertrude Bugler. Florence noted her husband's enthusiasm for Miss Bugler with her habitual tolerant amusement; "he is quite crazy about her," she wrote to a friend,[6] and linking this especially with Hardy's admiration for the photograph of the new young Mrs. Shorter, added, "I say there's safety in numbers."

On this occasion, it obviously never occurred to Florence (nor at any time to Gertrude Bugler herself) that there could be anything but safety in the aged author taking delight in the good looks and undoubted acting talent of such a young woman. Florence herself shared his delight. "She is a beautiful creature, only 24," she wrote, adding as a characteristic form of commendation, "really nice and refined." At the same time she noted jealousies among the other players as "Miss Bugler looking prettier than ever in her mumming dress" stole all the applause. "So you see it *is* possible to have too good a leading lady," she explained to no less a person than Sydney Cockerell, Director of the Fitzwilliam Museum.[7] These lighthearted, even naively innocent remarks were to come home to roost in the next few years. By 1922, Florence too was experiencing jealousy. She wrote an insulting letter to Miss Bugler, who had recently married a cousin, implying she lacked that "refinement" Florence formerly praised, and had in some mysterious way fallen short of "our station of life" at Max Gate.[8]

Worn and prematurely aged by her operation in October 1924, Florence returned to find Hardy in a seventh heaven at Gertrude Bugler's portrayal of his favourite heroine, Tess of the d'Urbervilles. In 4 December he wrote to his publisher[9] about a forthcoming specially illustrated limited edition of *Tess*.

> I think it would be a great help to the artist . . . to see the young woman who has personified Tess in the play, who is the very incarnation of her.

He enclosed tickets for extra performances at Weymouth. The artist, Mrs. Doyle Jones, attended, and Hardy wrote a letter to Mrs. Bugler (as she now was) in somewhat arch terms about the effect of her performance on the illustrator.

> Her face was so blurred with crying that she was ashamed to let us see her & ran off to the hotel. That was your doing, young lady! There were a good many wet handkerchiefs besides hers.

A photograph of the cast at a dinner given by the Mayor of Weymouth shows Gertrude Bugler, beautiful and radiant at Hardy's right hand. Florence sits on the far side of the Mayor, withdrawn into impenetrable gloom, and looking as if she is suffering deep depression.

Worse still, in this dangerous situation, Gertrude Bugler received an offer to play the part with a professional cast in London, and a point was reached when salaries and dates were fixed. From scattered letters it appears that Hardy at first did not fully wish her to leave Dorset, while Florence encouraged it, perhaps feeling that safety lay in separating her from Hardy. She suggested places to stay in London, and assured Gertrude Bugler that professional actresses with a young child (which Mrs. Bugler now had) managed to run their lives successfully. At some time after her own birthday, in mid-January 1925, when she said, she felt she was going mad, Florence's nerve broke. Preceded by an unintelligible telegram, she appeared on Gertrude Bugler's doorstep, announcing she was there without Hardy's knowledge. He had threatened to go and see Mrs. Bugler if she acted in London, and Florence now implored her to give up the part. In an alarming interview, she spoke wildly of a poem written by Hardy imagining an elopement between himself and Mrs. Bugler on Toller Down, where Hardy believed his own ancestors had originated. Florence claimed to have seized the poem and burnt it. Whether it existed in anything but her distraught imagination will never be known. Mrs. Bugler behaved, as she had always done, with instinctive and steady correctness. At great personal sacrifice, she renounced the part, and wrote to Hardy. They never communicated again, though her portrait appeared as Tess in the limited edition of 1926.

Florence had won a contest which was perhaps almost entirely imaginary. There is no doubt she was ill, as she confessed to friends. Her sister Connie, summoned urgently, came to stay. It was now she asserted her claim to Hardy's publishers that she should "write" Hardy's biography. Did she make this claim to give herself confidence that she was indeed mistress at Max Gate? She may also have wished to obviate any danger that Hardy himself would slip into her concocted life of him such episodes as had just occurred. It is certain that Mrs. Bugler was not the only person to receive violent and irrational attacks over this matter. "Please burn it & forgive & forget," she wrote[10] to Rebekah Owen, whom she had seen talking to Mrs. Bugler after a performance of *Tess*, and to whom she had written wildly. In August 1925, some months later, talking to Sydney Cockerell, she returned to the topic of Hardy's "infatuation".

What was the truth behind this incident? Mrs. Bugler remained convinced that Hardy was simply stirred by seeing his heroine come to life in her acting. Her Tess was "the very incarnation" of his imagination, as he had written to his publisher. Florence's version of the event, on the other hand, carefully prepared for friends such as Barrie,[11] was that Mrs. Bugler had herself decided to give up the part because of her husband and child. Florence's conduct therefore remains an enigma. Had her operation in October 1924 lowered her resistance to one of those attacks of depression she inherited from her mother? Were her accusations against Hardy—that he spoke roughly to her, neglected her birthday (12 January), and the bizarre incident of her burning the "elopement" poem—figments of her disordered nerves, or did they originate in actual behaviour by her husband? Nearly ten years before she had written of her "natural depression—or temper", leaving it open whether she could control its manifestations. Similarly now, though confessing to having suffered "a bad nervous illness", she claimed her conduct had been caused by some factual happenings.

What more happily seems to have emerged from this incident is an increase in her new-found, protective solicitude for her husband. After all, her excuse to Mrs. Bugler for blighting her hopes as an actress had been that Hardy would injure his health by going to performances in London, a type of journey he himself had renounced for good two years before. It is likely that, on reflection, the rather pathetic boyishness of his behaviour had brought out the vein of maternal tenderness which was such a feature of Florence's character. Henceforth she showed a protective sense devoid of any rancour, except against those who, she felt, had imposed upon him. She was, it is true, violently indignant against people who, invited to Max Gate, tried to make copy out of the experience by portraying Hardy as affected by age. "I hate", she afterwards wrote.[12] "any description of his personal appearance when he had grown old—baldness, wrinkles, etc." Visitors were carefully vetted so that their conversation and ideas should not upset Hardy, who, since 1920, had shown "a certain rigidity" about morals, politics, and social manners. Rutland Boughton slipped through her net, and discomfited Hardy by talking communism at him; but when he invited Florence to join the Party, she firmly shut him up, and "said I feared my husband would be worried and annoyed if I did so". As for women, she judged them now not with jealousy, but on the same grounds—would they in any way upset her husband? She agreed with Sassoon that one poet's wife would not be welcome to Hardy, though "I should be very pleased to see her". For the first time in all her marriage, she conquered her aversion to the Gifford family, and invited Gordon Gifford, his wife and ten-year-old daughter to come to meals at Max Gate, where Hardy, delighted, made much of the small girl, Emma's grand-niece. On another level of affectionate consideration, when the anti-social but much-loved dog Wessex died, Florence provided Hardy not with another dog, which she herself might have preferred, but with a kitten, such as the cat-loving Emma would have produced for him. She helped Hardy scrape the moss off Emma's gravestone, though she could not restrain one last cynicism, when Hardy, on the fifteenth anniversary of Emma's death, on 27 November 1927, wore a shabby little black hat—"very pathetic—all the more when one remembers what their married life was like".[13] Otherwise, her lips were henceforth sealed on her former violent expressions about her predecessor.

Shortly after, on 11 December 1927, Hardy became ill and exhausted. Though Florence blamed herself for letting an American publisher tire him, it was simply that his stubborn constitution, so well tended by her, was finally running down. Florence spent a month facing what had been a possibility ever since their marriage. She would lose him and be left alone, childless and purposeless. Sitting by herself on Christmas Day, her mind went back over all the Christmases she had known. She fixed on that of 1910 "especially". It was the last time she had known Alfred Hyatt alive at Enfield, though others from that time may have peopled her memories—

13 Hardy aged 86, drawn by Alfred Wollmark, 5 July 1926

Sir Thornley Stoker, newly widowed, Florence Henniker, newly met. Hardy was now too tired to read more than an occasional poem, such as de la Mare's *The Listeners*, though on 26 December they had a discussion about the Nativity, and agreed that there was not a grain of proof the Bible story was true. Heavy snow hemmed in the house, and visitors such as Cockerell and Barrie whispered of

Westminster Abbey. Eva was there to do much of the nursing and watching, aided by a reliable parlour-maid obtained at last, Nellie Titterington. Florence read to him—all poems now—from Browning's *Rabbi Ben Ezra*, and a verse from the *Rubaiyat*, out of the book that had been his present to her. It was Eva who, on 11 January, heard his last cry, "Eva, Eva, what is this?" Though Florence watched by him till death, he did not speak again.

13

"So Futile and Hopeless"

ALTHOUGH it was a crisis Florence long had anticipated—she confided[1] to a trusted servant, "I did not think Mr. Hardy was going to live as long as he has"—the event of Hardy's death seemed to find her utterly unprepared. Her appearance and behaviour correspond with T. E. Lawrence's estimate that she would be like a pot-plant which had suddenly been deprived of its surrounding flowerpot. She somehow got through the Westminster Abbey ceremony, though with her own doctor from Dorchester in close attendance, and on the firm arm of Sydney Cockerell. Already her first days of widowhood had been savaged by controversy. The Abbey burial had been entirely the idea of Cockerell, with his lieutenant Barrie, who had used his charm on the Dean. Neither seemed to realize that Hardy wished to lie among the family graves he had so often taken Florence to visit in Stinsford churchyard. She knew, but was persuaded by the overbearing Cockerell, a matter of bitter regret all the rest of her life. She found it alienated at once Hardy's brother and sister, Henry and Kate. Once more over-persuaded, this time by the Stinsford vicar, she consented to let Hardy's heart be buried separately in the churchyard where he had wished his body to be. To her horror, she found that this too caused disgust, not only in Dorchester, but among Hardy's relatives and oldest friends, some of whom found it repellent. A surgeon was summoned, and a gruesome operation took place, giving rise to grim, bucolic legends, still current. Even the Abbey ceremony caused its controversy, which led the Dean to write privately to the incumbent of the parish in which Max Gate lay, to be reassured over Hardy's beliefs and moral behaviour.

Grappling with something substantial to do for Hardy's memory, harassed by Cockerell, who started, unauthorized, a claim that Hardy wished for a large-scale memorial in or near his native Dorchester, Florence clutched at the self-imposed fiction of presenting Hardy's third-person autobiography as her biography. It was, of course, virtually ready, but in the interests of probability, she let only a first part be published in 1928, covering the years up to *Tess*. In the next few months between Hardy's death and publication, she set one individual mark upon it. Her obsessive denigration of Emma, and of anything to do with the family and name of Gifford, had ceased over the later part of Hardy's life. She was pleased that Emma's nephew Gordon attended the Stinsford heart-burial, and laid an annual wreath on the grave. Yet, as she read through the concocted work, soon to appear under her name, her "temper", as she called it, rose over Hardy's eagerness to record in its pages every single incident favourable to his first wife, her courage, her decision, her help, her social successes, together with examples of his own affection for Emma. She red-pencilled out of the typescript nearly every one of these incidents and expressions. Out went a long passage describing Emma's bravery in rescuing Hardy from a street-attack by thieves in Rome, during the Hardys' visit there in 1887. She deleted equally long descriptions of successful lunch-parties given by Emma. Any sign of Hardy's retrospective tolerance of his first wife's religious beliefs was likewise removed, including the innocuous sentence, "his wife was an old-fashioned Evangelical like her mother". One of Florence's first attractions for Hardy had been her own *un*belief. She could not stomach his tacit acceptance of the rival whose ideas she had hoped to supplant.

As she went on to revise the second volume, *The Later Years*, there was one other deception she could not bring herself to countenance as the apparent author of the work. This was the fiction, so elaborately and continuously planted by Hardy, that her own acquaintance with Emma, of barely two years, somehow constituted a long-standing friendship and shared intimacy. Hardy's totally false description[2] of herself as one

who had been for several years the friend of the first Mrs. Hardy, and had accompanied her on the little excursions she had liked to make when her husband could not go,

was firmly crossed out in the interests of the truth known to such people as Edward Clodd. Clodd knew that Florence's many "little excursions" to his home at Aldeburgh had been taken not with Emma but with Hardy, many at dates before Emma knew of Florence's existence, and had been arranged, in Clodd's own words, so that there should be no chance of "Emma intervening". Striving for some semblance of truth in the web of deception she had evolved, she even denied her one genuine excursion with Emma, when in 1911 "Mrs. Hardy, accompanied by her friend Miss Dugdale went to stay at Worthing". Her introduction to Max Gate in 1910 as "Miss Dugdale, a literary friend of Mrs. Hardy's at the Lyceum Club", implied that Emma, not Hardy, met her first; her essentially truthful nature, though hopelessly distorted by the weird conditions of her marriage, was unable to acquiesce. The passage was crossed out, together with its circumstantial continuation, claiming that her Dorset ancestors had once lived near the Hardys, "and had married with them some 130 years earlier'', an event unrecorded in any register other than Hardy's own wishful fantasy.

There were innumerable other difficulties of her new position. Hardy had named her as joint trustee with Sydney Cockerell, with particular instruction to destroy matter relating to his earlier life. Florence, it has been said, destroyed many early letters and notes. It seems likely, however, that Hardy had already done this, in the fine sifting he had carried out methodically while writing his autobiography. He left behind only two little shiny black memorandum books, into which he had copied very brief notes from his diaries and notebooks from past years. What Florence is known to have destroyed is every possible trace at Max Gate of Emma. The long years of living with Emma's two locked attic boudoirs, kept exactly as they were when she died in them, had weighed heavily on Florence's married life. Four years before Hardy's death, she had described to Louisa Yearsley the Bluebeard incubus of these rooms, crammed with old clothes, cardboard boxes of Emma's writings, every sort of junk, and had, she said, sometimes longed for Max Gate to be burnt down, "without anyone being injured. But what an awful remedy.''[3] Now, with the help of the gardener she could make this happen by carrying out the entire contents to the garden, and setting light to it in bonfire pyres. Everything, including even Emma's old corsets, is remembered as going up in the flames.

One other thing she would have liked to remove was by now her co-trustee. Cockerell's letter to *The Times*, about a Hardy Memorial, appeared side by side with an account of the Abbey funeral. Claiming that Hardy would have approved of something like the seventy-foot column, which already celebrated the other Hardy, Nelson's captain, it deeply shocked her. She was morbidly sensitive to anything that seemed the slightest slur on her husband's last days. The idea that the reticent man should be presented as wishing to dominate in death the Dorset landscape was strangely abhorrent. A complicated wrangle broke out, similar to that which marked the burial. Cockerell was all for the grandiose, Henry and Kate all for the simple, with Florence on their side, and Barrie darting from camp to camp. Moreover, Cockerell's domineering manner over the literary remains shocked her. Already he was showing, with Hardy dead, a contempt for her which he afterwards expressed by calling her "an inferior woman with a suburban mind". She even wanted to wash her hands of the whole affair. "It all seems so futile and hopeless,'' she wrote in May to Siegfried Sassoon,[4] on taking the initiative, disapproved by Cockerell, of giving the manuscript of Hardy's posthumous book of poems to Queen's College, Oxford, where he had been an honorary fellow. Two months later, after "a

perfectly awful time" with Cockerell, she wished to resign her
trusteeship, but was dissuaded by Daniel Macmillan, the publisher.

For yet another burden on her conscience was the projected biography, to appear as quickly as feasible under her name. "I was very
rushed by publishers & the agent about the first volume of the biography, which is now [May] in the printer's hands."[5] Perhaps as a
reaction to the deception she knew she was about to practise, she
lashed out at other writers, who, she felt, had tried to cash in on
Hardy's death by giving newspaper impressions of Hardy in his later
years, and who "calmly cabled off to America for money ... Oh,
my God *no*!" Sassoon attempted to calm her after she had written
a specially virulent attack[6] on H. M. Tomlinson for his article in the
Saturday Review of Literature. In a month she was miserably con-
trite.[7] "I would give worlds to unwrite that letter if it were possible,
for I was completely in the wrong." Thanks probably to Sassoon,
the breach with the good-natured and talented Tomlinson was
healed after another two years had passed, but by that time another
offender had appeared, Robert Graves, with his reminiscences, *Good-
Bye to All That*. He had tried to be anecdotal and amusing about
his visit to Max Gate, but "I so dislike", wrote Florence,[8] "that way
of describing T.H. as a rather comic old gentleman." Sassoon was
again her confidant, but he, to match his sexual ambiguity, of which
Florence seems to have been totally unaware, played an ambiguous
role in his correspondence with her. He sympathized, advised, gently
corrected her. Yet at the same time he was reporting her vagaries
of judgment to Cockerell, a fact of which the latter was only too
apt to take full advantage. Her attitude toward the handsome
Sassoon remained, to the end, pathetically humble, even when she
suspected his attitude to her had its reservations. When he sent
her, with some trepidation, his own poem *Max Gate*, which could be
interpreted as criticizing her own over-protective management
of Hardy—

> Hardy, the Wessex wizard, wasn't there.
> Good care was taken to keep him out of sight ...

Florence wrote back, perhaps only half-understanding the full impli-
cation of the verses, "So far from being hurt or offended I am grateful
to you for having written it."[9] As for herself, when Volume I of her
so-called biography of Hardy came out, she confessed, "I hadn't the
courage to send you a copy." Did she suspect that he, like T. E.
Lawrence and Barrie, knew too much about how the work had been
produced?

"It will be regarded by many as a dull book—a failure in fact,"
she wrote despondently to Sassoon. In fact, when *The Early Life
of Thomas Hardy* appeared on 2 November 1928, the reviews hardly

bore out her pessimistic forecasts. Most of them were not only respectful but enthusiastic. Desmond MacCarthy and Hugh Walpole gave it praise; others found it "reticent", but rightly so, like Hardy's own "reticence", commended by Quiller-Couch in his Cambridge lectures. The main criticism was that it did not reveal enough of Hardy's philosophic attitudes, a lack that Florence could hardly have supplied, even if she had been allowed to insert them.

Florence's feelings as she read these opinions must have been complicated in the extreme. Did she really, as she afterwards wrote to Sassoon, "suppose people think that a man's widow is the wrong person to write his biography"? For that, of course, was precisely what she had *not* done. The deception, into which she had been lured by Hardy during his life, was having posthumous consequences of extreme puzzlement. It almost seems she began to believe that she had, in some sense, written the book. Certainly her self-confidence, never great, needed bolstering up in the literary position she now so strangely occupied. It began to be sadly apparent that many literary people had mainly tolerated her not for herself but as an adjunct to Hardy. Sydney Cockerell was beginning to be almost openly contemptuous of her judgment and taste in matters of literature. In 1929, she rescued and made one of her private printings of a neglected story by Hardy, *Old Mrs. Chundle.* She found Cockerell publicly furious that he had not been consulted. His friends, such as T. E. Lawrence, assumed Cockerell was the sole arbiter over which poems and stories by Hardy should be preserved, sinking Florence in virtual nonentity. When, in 1932, a church was reconsecrated as a memorial to Hardy, everyone forgot to ask her, "poor F.H.".[10]

In point of fact, when her second volume, strategically delayed until the spring of 1930, appeared once more above her name, its general reception would have been almost entirely gratifying to anyone else; but Florence was depressedly determined to be self-deprecatory about the whole affair. Yet even this attitude was seized by some reviewers as praiseworthy in the book itself. The phrase "discreet and reticent" was used in commendation, and even recognized as characteristic of the "author". It was indeed commented that this had gone at times too far, making the book a "record" rather than a "biography", and in one place it was acutely noticed how Florence's personal relationship with her late husband was altogether omitted. Yet, in several instances, the reaction was more than gratifying. Osbert Burdett, in the influential *London Mercury*, summed up both volumes as "admirable". The *New York Book Review* went further, and said that the double volume formed "one of the most distinguished biographies anywhere to be found". There is nothing in any review to justify Florence's gloomy verdict to Sassoon that her work had been "a dire failure".

One of the definite handicaps arising from publication was, though, that Florence had now sedulously to maintain not only the prime fiction about its authorship, and the omission of certain aspects of Hardy's life—her "reticences"—but also multiple fictions of omission and suppression relating to her own past life. This is the period of her almost total suppression of her long early career as an elementary school teacher. She got into the habit of pretending that though she had written children's books (discreetly never quoted) she had small knowledge of children, nor any past opportunity to know about them. The rough but appreciative boys in the crowded classes at St. Andrew's, Enfield, were banished from her official history as if they had not existed.

Already, her new public status as Hardy's approved biographer generally confirmed, she saw herself at Max Gate, about which she had so often and so bitterly complained, as the priestess in charge of a shrine. The dining-room was arranged virtually as his memorial. A frank description exists, written by a woman who was, in the 1930s, running a small typewriting agency in Dorchester, and whom Florence called in to help with a projected but never completed collection of Hardy's main correspondence.[11]

> The room resembled an overcrowded museum. Tall bookcases had been erected round the walls and two-tiered ones under the window-sills. The panes of glass were small and the stone pillars large, thus obstructing the light. In each bookcase were rows and rows of the volumes written by Mr. Hardy and translated into many languages ... Over the mantelpiece hung a painting of Thomas Hardy in his university robes that he wore when receiving an honorary degree; a photograph, rather smaller, stood on the top of one bookcase and several photographs, taken at an early age, stood in frames on the top of other bookcases. There was also a bust of his head and a miniature of the author beside it. The whole atmosphere brought Mr. Hardy to life, and one felt surrounded by his presence: it was almost stifling.

This is the atmosphere, created with uncanny accuracy by Somerset Maugham in *Cakes and Ale*, which "seemed so strangely dead; it had already the mustiness of a museum". Fortunately for Florence, there were other elements in her widowhood than the role of the supposititious biographer of a great man. She was enabled to have a life of her own, even at the expense of problems that beset her new and isolated position with fresh instances of tragi-comical futility.

14

"Time and Her Friends"

WRITING to Sydney Cockerell, T. E. Lawrence professed himself puzzled by the provisions in Hardy's will.[1]

> I hope Mrs. Hardy will console herself with time and her friends ...
> It seems she may not be well off. The royalties (after a spurt this year
> and next) will run away very small in the next 20 years. I gather that
> beyond that she has only £600 a year.

Lawrence was entirely wrong. The annuity of £600 seemed a fortune to Florence, after being kept all her married life on an income so small that she had to raid Sir Thornley Stoker's legacy to make up the housekeeping. Hardy in fact left an estate valued at over £90,000. In modern terms he was a millionaire, a fact which caused much local cynicism, when it was remembered that his idea of a post-man's Christmas Box had been one small coin, a sixpence. Florence, who had to make up, again out of her own income, the servants' presents and tradesmen's tips, found that all along she had been married to a wealthy man. Nor could Lawrence have been more in error about Hardy's royalties and copyrights, also bequeathed to her, "my most prized possession", as she came to call them. Far from "running away very small", Hardy's works, over fifty years, have never lost their popularity: indeed it has noticeably increased. The royalties and copyrights were a gold-mine to Florence during her widowhood, and to her legatees after her own death. In spite of the annoyance, distress, and even, as she said, humiliation suffered in hav-ing to consult Cockerell over these matters, she was now the pos-sessor of a rich inheritance. In the early years of her marriage she had proclaimed that she cared nothing for money. Now, after Hardy's surprisingly long-delayed death, she was reaping an un-expected harvest of wealth.

With the innate generosity which was always Florence's most win-ning feature, she at once wondered if she could use the new income to help the neighbours who, she felt, needed it most. Henry and Kate Hardy, she knew, were well-found, with their substantial house, Talbothays, and Henry's numerous real-estate properties in the dis-trict. Florence had often worried about their surviving Hardy cousin, Teresa, aged eighty-five, and living in eccentric seclusion with a colony of cats in Lower Bockhampton. She had suggested helping her during Hardy's lifetime, only to be told gruffly not to interfere in Hardy family matters. Now, before Florence could make enquiries, Teresa followed her famous cousin to the grave. To her horror, Florence found that the uncompromising old lady, who thought Tom should never have written books, had died in abject poverty.[2] Florence felt that the well-known Hardy clannishness had frustrated her innocent desire to help. A luckier chance gave her means to make up for an occasion when she herself had been far from innocent in inflicting a wrong. Gertrude Bugler had attended Hardy's heart-burial with a wreath inscribed from "the sorrowing woman", who had created the stage Tess, but who had been robbed of her London appearance by Florence's jealous intervention. Hearing that a London revival, prompted by Hardy's death, was imminent, Florence used her influence (and perhaps money) as Hardy's literary executor to insist the management offered the part to Mrs. Bugler. The two women, with Hardy dead, met as friends. Mrs. Bugler returned to her the half-crazed letter Florence had written on the former unhappy occasion, and, with her own generous and forgiving nature, accepted the part. Her London début, with an all-professional cast, was a triumph; her name appeared in lights as "Hardy's Own Tess".

In using Hardy's legacies to do good, intended or actual, Florence did not neglect her own need to make up for some of the deprivations forced on her by the extraordinary conditions of her marriage. Three of her ambitions had been to own a car, with her personal chauffeur, to visit Europe (America even), and to have a flat of her own in London. In July 1928, she bought an Austin Twelve, engaged a local driver, Dick Shipton, and installed him in a small house in Monmouth Road, Dorchester.[3] She was in 1930 able to accept the Hanbury's invitation to their beautiful villa, La Mortola, on the Italian Riviera. Yet she found herself handicapped by her intensely local and narrow experience, confined to provincial life, first at Enfield, then at Dorchester; she had earlier refused a similar invitation from the "angelic" Max Beerbohms at Rapallo on the grounds that she had never before been abroad. Although she was offered a lecture tour in the U.S.A. in 1930, after the *Life* was completed, her dream of a visit to America was never achieved. For one thing, Barrie advised against the arduousness of a tour, though recommending a visit.

However, the third and perhaps deepest of her dreams of self-fulfilment was the earliest to be achieved in her new-found and well-funded widowhood. The idea of a flat in London had been an ambition ever since, far back in 1910, she had been lent the apartment near Baker Street. It had been a topic to which she had reverted all through her married life, even ousting the idea that she might live near her beloved father at Brighton. A trip in the 1920s to the rapidly-growing sprawl of that seaside resort had proved disillusioning. London, however, the hub of the literary and social world, still held its magic, just as it had done earlier in the century for the young, down-trodden elementary school teacher from Enfield. To live in the very centre, with no need for the hideous journey back home through the northern suburbs, had been a prime ambition in her life, to have at any rate the outward circumstances of what Hardy had called "the modern intelligent, mentally emancipated young woman of cities".[4]

So, by the Michaelmas Quarter 1928, barely nine months after the death of a husband whose age and needs had banished her from the delights of the capital, Florence was installed in her flat at 8 Adelphi Terrace. She described it as

> a little flat in the same house ... where my husband worked. I chose this flat because it is the only house in London that is clearly associated with him.[5]

The flat had almost certainly been obtained through James Barrie, who lived in the next block, Adelphi Terrace House, and who would be a very welcome neighbour. For some reason her lease of No. 8 proved unsatisfactory, and fell through after nine months, but she was happy there, and returned a few years later to another flat in the same terrace, No. 5, a place with other and older artistic associations. The actor Garrick had lodged here. "I write this", she informed Paul Lemperly, the Ohio book-collector,[6] with whom she exchanged letters until her death, "in the room where Garrick died."

Luckily Florence, and for that matter Barrie also, were on their own death-beds during the final acts of municipal vandalism which destroyed the old Adelphi Terrace. Her dwelling here was a pleasure which compensated for some of her experiences at Max Gate. She is known to have looked supremely happy, without a trace of what was called her "Max Gate look".[7] Lady Cynthia Asquith, visiting Max Gate for the first time had, indeed, somewhat unkindly said that Florence was "no prettier than the house". In Adelphi Terrace her looks and spirits revived. Instead of the five uncanny owls, hooting dismally, which used to peer weirdly at night-time through the Max Gate windows, there was now the enchanted view at dusk of the Thames, "all the world a trembling blue light", the mysterious ships, and the electric signs along the Victoria Embankment, gleaming in the river. Even the whisky advertisement of a Scots soldier in full uniform had its own peculiar charm. A kindly cockney housekeeper, in charge of the block, would climb the four or five flights—there was no lift—to see that the fragile-looking "poor dear from

Dorset" was well and happy. The housekeeper's seven-year-old son was fascinating to Florence, with her love of small male children. He was urbanly independent, and even at his age could teach her all the short cuts through the little alleyways of that still-confusing neighbourhood.[8]

Nor was Florence alone there. She now had what she had always desired, her own personal maid. Nellie Titterington, the sensible parlour-maid at Max Gate, who had helped Eva Dugdale to nurse Hardy in his last illness, consented to take the post of living-in maid with Florence in London. She was someone Florence could trust, and perhaps was a relief to talk to. With Nellie she could drop her role as the great writer's widow. Together they made expeditions to the shops, crowded, sometimes frightening, always intriguing. Florence even explored with Nellie the territory of the 1930s down-and-outs, who slept under newspapers and rags along the Embankment. She had dresses made or altered by the wife of Gordon Gifford, who had married a qualified dressmaker, and not, as Florence had contemptuously thought and repeated, "a waitress in a tea-shop" or "his tea-shop girl".[9] Florence was now, it seems, happier with women of the class she herself had originally come from, however much she hid her origins from the world.

She was, in fact, and in spite of her long apprenticeship at Max Gate, desperately out of her depth in the world of successful literature and of the upper middle classes generally. Nothing shows this more clearly than what now occurred between Florence and her new neighbour, Sir James Barrie. Florence had come to feel that, over the years, she had got to know Barrie well. They had exchanged letters since the year before her marriage. By the time of her death, she accumulated nearly a hundred and fifty letters[10] from the strange little Scottish baronet, who had risen in the world from a weaver's cottage, much as Hardy had done from his Bockhampton hamlet. These letters by Barrie were couched, especially after Hardy's death, in what Florence felt to be intimate and even affectionate terms. Even before the death, he had practised his boyish charm gambit. "I forget if I ever told you how much I like you. No, too shy, but I do like you very much." Now his praise of her as the erstwhile partner of a great man, "to whom you are indeed a great wife", was poetically fulsome. A week after Hardy's burial he wrote

> I think the heart that is now at Stinsford had been calling long and bleakly for what you were at last to do for him. I honour you very much.

He guaranteed to go to her at any time that she thought he might be of the slightest service. He offered his Adelphi flat at any moment "where you would be absolutely secluded". When she got her own flat in Adelphi Terrace, he welcomed her unreservedly.

When she moved in, his letters, all now beginning "My dear Florence", became even more affectionately playful and personal.

> I am so glad you are sleeping well at last. We might have a string between the two flats, so that when you tugged I could send the sleeping draught bottle down it.

In fact when he himself fell ill early in 1929, she spent long hours nursing him, and won his thanks for "the help you were to me when you stayed those nights". On his side, Barrie rallied Florence on her lack of self-confidence and her moods of chronic despondency. "I wish you were not so highly-strung ... If you did not keep it under control so much you would suffer less from it." He noted kindly "the self-distrust that so often floods you, and is so uncalled for and yet is, I admit, an endearing part of you". He wrote, apropos of her *Life* of Hardy, that she had been what he called Hardy's "vol. 2 ... triumph enough for any woman".

There was enough, in such letters, for the fifty-year-old still-unsophisticated Florence to have daydreams about her relationship with this newly-assiduous friend. Barrie was now in his early seventies, the exact age Hardy had been when she married him. He apparently needed looking after, always a great point with the sympathetic Florence; for, in spite of a valet, housekeeper, and two lady secretaries, his overwhelming bronchial cough and agonizing chest often reduced him to a painful state, for which his doctor's only prescription was heroin. He would be no trouble sexually, not only because of his age, but because, as his one marriage had shown, he was impotent. Like Hardy he was mother-fixated, searching for a Mrs. Darling, like his own Peter Pan. Florence began to play the part of more than just a neighbour. She gave him a little Persian-style rug, worked for him with her own hands. She sent weekly boxes of new-laid eggs from her once-derided hens, her Max Gate flowers, her new-grown tender carrots, delivered to Barrie by Nellie Titterington and the chauffeur, Dick Shipton. She herself went to tea and dinner with him frequently. When he could make the breathless climb, unaided by any lift, to her flat, she took special care of his entertainment, with his favourite meals, soup, fish, cutlets, apple tart and cream, "the latter a great favourite of Sir James", made according to Nellie's Dorset recipe. After dinner, they were left together, with the wine on the sideboard, "to have a little chat". There was no doubt where Florence hoped all this would lead. Nellie Titterington shrewdly observed, "She was a happy person in those days. I knew it would please her very much if she could become Lady Barrie."[11] Fatally, she ignored George Bernard Shaw's

commonsense, cheerful advice:[12] "Don't marry another genius ...
Marry somebody who has nothing else to do than to take care of
you." Florence, with her inexperience and limited background, had
no knowledge what hopeless disappointment she was building for
herself.

Though she had known Barrie, in her capacity of Hardy's wife,
for nearly fifteen years, she had no inkling that she was dealing with
a creature even more complex than her late husband. This type of
situation was no new thing in Barrie's life, and was well-known to
his principal secretary, Cynthia Asquith, who wrote[13] that

> he was apt to make himself much too charming to casually-met
> strangers, thus raising hopes of a lasting intimacy—hopes he had no
> time to satisfy. Again and again, I would see him caught in a web
> of his own weaving.

Though Florence was more than a casually-met stranger, she had
been met by Barrie through her husband, Hardy. That too was an
appalling danger for her widowed state. Barrie had a need to over-
whelm the widows of men he admired with the wildest attentions
and flattery. His notes to Florence on her "great biography" pale
beside some of his statements to the widow of Scott of the Antarctic.
His pursuit of Lady Scott was so publicly excessive that she actually
had to write to the news editor of the *Daily Chronicle* denying that,
after her husband's death, she had secretly married Barrie.[14]

With attractive married women, not yet widowed, Barrie's pro-
ceedings were even more remarkable. He simply moved in, sometimes literally into their houses, and claimed possession of themselves, their husbands, and children. The Asquiths had to share their
married life, Herbert Asquith often in revolt, with this tiny, persistent, monopolizing genius. Even richer, and ten times more charming
than Hardy, he was not above using large money presents when
charm failed. His generosity would have been attractive, if it had
not had this huge element of emotional self-interest. Such possessive-
ness infected his whole entourage. Cynthia Asquith, apt to receive
presents of £500 over and above her large secretarial salary, was
naturally suspiciously jealous of any women other than her friend
and co-helper, Mrs. E. V. Lucas. She saw Florence's unsuspecting
interest as a menace, and noted in her diary that Barrie had over-
done the compliments on Hardy's death, and was now paying for
them. Florence was becoming "portentous", and actually rebuking
herself and Mrs. Lucas for calling Barrie "Jimmie", and for not
behaving with a due sense of reverence.[15]

Once again, Florence had entered a world and a society of whose
intricate inner rules she had only a surface knowledge. Her carefully
planned, intimate little dinners meant nothing to the hero of a

14   Sir James Barrie at the unveiling of the Hardy Memorial, 2 September
1931

hundred aristocratic house-parties. True to form, the more bored
he became with her, the more flattering his remarks. He unveiled
the Hardy statue for her at Dorchester on 2 September 1931, and
managed a typical indirect compliment. "I feel sure T.H. was
pleased with you on the 2nd. September." There arose a time when
such "dewdrops", as Cynthia Asquith called the extravagantly insincere expressions of admiration, had to cease. What exactly
occurred is unsure. Sydney Cockerell, by now in open warfare with

Florence, later said, with typical malice, that Barrie actually proposed to her, and then, woundingly, withdrew his proposal.[16] Much that Cockerell said in extreme old age can be proved false; Barrie, at any time, was too wily a bird for such a pantomime. Yet, overnight, something happened. The visits and presents abruptly ceased. Nellie Titterington was told to cancel her tea-appointment with Barrie's valet and housekeeper. Florence packed for Dorset; "the Max Gate look" was on her face once more.

Perhaps something similar occurred in Florence's relationship with Siegfried Sassoon, to whom Barrie had once referred, writing to Florence, as "your favourite Sassoon (I am jealous of that youth!)". Her letters to Sassoon become more and more pathetically insecure. "When are you going to enter this gate again?" she wrote on 19 December 1932. When he married, under a year later, her letter of congratulation was tragically humble. "I have made many mistakes in the past, & no doubt have forfeited your friendship, but I am always grateful for what I had of that & think of you with affection & deepest regard."[17] The nuances of society's and literature's aristocrats had bewildered Florence. Tolerated, even liked, while her husband was alive, she too often found herself shrugged off after his death. Yet she still had her place in the world of literature, and achieved some use there, if only on a minor scale.

Shortly after Hardy's death, Sydney Cockerell and Barrie had discussed the question of publishing Hardy's letters. Both agreed the ideal editor would be Edmund Gosse with (Florence's suggestion) Sassoon as assistant.[18] Unfortunately Gosse died later in the year. Florence did not feel capable of editing them herself, especially with the contemptuous estimate of her worth held by Cockerell. She had, however, a collection which formed a considerable responsibility. In 1923, on Mrs. Henniker's death, Hardy's letters to her had been returned, by her wish, to Max Gate. They were followed in 1928 by Hardy's letters to Gosse, also on the death of the recipient. Then there were the letters not to but *from* Barrie. True to form, Barrie had largely written by the oblique method of addressing Florence, thus maintaining unique personal contact with the wife of a great man. There were all these, locked in the desks and drawers of Max Gate. Surely something should be done with them.

Florence determined at least to put them into more durable form. She engaged the owner of a small typing agency in Dorchester to make typed copies. Adding the letters Hardy received from Gosse to those Hardy himself had written, she thus preserved a remarkable two-way exchange, lasting nearly fifty years. The correspondence with Mrs. Henniker was likewise made safe. They were joined by the 147 letters from Barrie to Florence herself. The originals of these have had a curious history. When Florence herself died, her effects were left to her sister Eva, to preserve or otherwise, as she thought fit. Eva, a hospital sister, made decisions on purely personal grounds. She retained the originals of only twenty-five letters. These mostly date from around the time of Hardy's death, when Barrie, characteristically, had been most fulsome about the merits of the newly-widowed Florence. The remaining 122, some of great general interest, were indiscriminately put up for sale. Yet happily, the full 147, in Florence's typescript copy, found their way to the Dorset County Museum, where they are today. Florence's care has benefited, as she intended, future scholars and enquirers.[19]

One of Florence's chief pleasures during her later years of life was the entertainment of American academic visitors. Young, deferential and with charming manners these graduate students and junior professors came to worship and study at the shrine she had created. To help their research and investigation into the association copies and manuscripts she allowed them to see, they were permitted to stay for nights at Max Gate, and absorb its atmosphere of reverential gloom. Sympathetically responding to appreciation, she even gave them documents and letters. It is clear that they, in their turn, had no inkling of her background. She appeared to them the gracious lady in a somewhat Henry James type of story. On the other hand, if any American were rash or brash enough to encroach on her copyrights, Florence showed her old spirit. When Professor Carl J. Weber reprinted Hardy's *Indiscretions of an Heiress* in 1935, Florence got the Oxford University Press to refuse to distribute it in this country. "Professor Weber", she wrote,[20] "is a stranger to me", and she indignantly said that his edition made her feel "as if someone had been picking my pocket".[21] He was never allowed to visit Max Gate and meet her, though this did not prevent him, after her death, from writing as if he had known her well, and relating circumstantial anecdotes about herself and Hardy.

Yet it was not, ultimately, in literary or scholarly circles that Florence's years of widowhood were most usefully spent. The will o' the wisp of literary life, to which she had devoted so many years of agonizing attention, gave way to solid achievement of a very real and permanent kind, and formed what is perhaps her most enduring memorial.

15

"Coin of Another Realm"

THOMAS HARDY had roundly condemned his first wife because she "ran after local people" in Dorchester. Florence herself had been dubious about those who tried to exploit Hardy's reputation by running after him. Yet any suspicions she may have had, or any prohibitions imposed by her somewhat domineering husband, had melted at the genuine warmth and affection shown to her as his widow. A local inhabitant, speaking frankly of his fellow-townsmen's opinion, has said that "dislike of her husband did not rub off on her". Dorchester, in spite of its reputation for stubborn caution, was ready to welcome her for herself alone. Warm-hearted, though long suppressed, she was ready to respond.

This response could now be a generous one, in every sense. Hardy's death had left her, to her surprise, a really rich woman. How should she use these riches? As one who had suffered so frequently and frighteningly from ill-health, her mind at once turned to the needs of the local hospital. The Dorset General Hospital was a small and busy institution, raising money for its own keep by workmen's subscription schemes, donations, dances, entertainments, whist drives and a hospital ball. Local subscription played a leading part. Hardy, to the end of his life, had subscribed only one guinea per annum; many other citizens of Dorchester gave two, three, four, even five guineas. Florence at once took over his subscription, raised it to four guineas a year, and also subscribed to the Linen Guild. In the following year, 1929, she increased the subscription again to five guineas, and became thereby a Vice-Patron. Indirectly, her patronage benefited her own faithful parlour-maid, Nellie Titterington, who was an in-patient for some time in 1931.[1]

In an old-style voluntary hospital, such as this, much was done by its unpaid committee of management. In summer 1932 Florence appeared as a member of this body. Its members served on a regular rota as "visitors", generally for a month's duration each, so that there was always a representative available to sign cheques, supervise accounts, receive complaints, and, if necessary, take action in emergency on behalf of the committee. Florence served her first spell that autumn, while in the following year she appeared on the weekly board of management, which dealt with mundane but necessary details, such as contracts of milk and groceries, and deciding whether to use coke or boiler nuts for the hot-water system.

With the strong nursing influence in her own family, through her sister Eva, and her own care of elderly people such as Lady Stoker, Florence began in 1933 to turn her particular attention to the nursing staff and its training. She had, too, the inspiring example, over twenty-five years before, of her much loved Sir Thornley Stoker and his Dublin nursing school. At the end of the previous year, a sub-committee had reported on the "inadequacy of nursing staff", and put forward a scheme to attract more probationers and persuade them to stay. On the other hand, as the report on that year commented, the hospital was suffering from the effects of the general trade depression, which made people cautious over laying out money in voluntary efforts without financial return. Extreme economy in all departments was urged. Florence, however, with the accumulated Hardy capital and high copyright fees, was not affected, and used her money accordingly to attract nurses. In June, she presented a set of desks and chairs to the nurses' lecture room. In July she presented a refrigerator in working order. In October she served on the committee of the new nurses' home, for which she had successfully campaigned, though it was not in fact opened for two and a half years; she met with the architect and several firms of builders. She was well aware of the human side to this exacting profession, and showed this by a particularly thoughtful act. In December she saw that, at her suggestion, nurses successful in examinations should be presented with their medals in public, and their names inscribed on a board in the nurses' dining-room. At every stage she saw that there was no penny-pinching over the new home, arguing against a local councillor, who claimed "the proposed home represented luxury". Florence denied that the nurses could be put in sleeping cubicles, to save money, rather than in separate rooms. "Nurses work hard," she said, "and therefore require good accommodation."[2]

To take another aspect of Dorchester life, it will be recalled that Florence had been since 1924 a Borough Magistrate. She had thus taken a position which Hardy, in his last few years, had felt too old to occupy. At first, and during his remaining lifetime, it might seem from the Petty Sessions Minute Book that she "plays", as Hardy said of himself, "the part of Justice Silence with great assiduity." This is probably, however, misleading, since not only do the minutes seldom record a remark by an individual Justice, but Florence, according to her own letters, was often quite ill during the first year of her office. This accounts for her hardly attending at all in 1924, and with gaps in the years 1925–7, when Hardy's increasing weakness may also have made her unwilling to leave Max Gate for long sessions.

Her chief and very considerable contribution came with the

15   Florence in the last year of her life

Children's and Young Persons' Act of 1933, which was the basis of all subsequent legislation on child welfare. This Act defined wilful cruelty and neglect, restricted employment of children (particularly in street trading), extended Juvenile Courts to the age of seventeen and to "care and protection" cases, transferred Remand Homes to the local authority, and defined the responsibilities of Approved Schools and Probation Officers. Florence already, on 28 June 1933, when the Justices had received the report of the Probation Officer on girl offenders, had successfully moved that a special magistrates' meeting should be held to consider probation cases only. Denied children herself, inhibited, by a curious exercise of social shame, from admitting that she had been, for fourteen years of her fifty-four, an elementary school teacher, she still retained the love and care for children she had shown then to the deprived boys in some of the classes at Enfield.

Her activities with her fellow-Justices brought her in close contact with the realities of child welfare. On 10 July 1933, a husband and wife were fined for neglecting three children under four years old, and a week later the children were sent under court order to Dr.

Barnardo's. On 13 October, Florence was elected to serve on the special panel of magistrates for the juvenile court. Later that year she attended a conference at the Dorset County Council on the working of the new Children's and Young Persons' Act, in co-operation with the N.S.P.C.C., school attendance officers, health visitors, and the welfare committee. In the following year her activities in this field ranged from licensing thirty-five children to act in a pantomime to a case where a woman keeping a brothel was also suspected of ill-treating a child. The woman was now serving three months' hard labour for this previous offence, and Florence and the other magistrates made an order for her boy to be placed in a Dr. Barnardo's home until the age of eighteen. On the other hand, mindless brutality by children themselves exercised her sympathies while sitting on the bench. Kicking and beating cows in the market was frequent. Her work on the probation committee, to which she was elected in summer 1935, also brought her sadly in touch with the unhappy sides of life.[3]

Many of the offences, including that of the brothel-keeper's ill-treatment of her boy, came from the notorious Mill Street area. Florence Hardy's chief contribution to Dorchester, and one over which she clearly found most fulfilment in her later years, was her work for the Mill Street Housing Society. Mill Street was the infamous "Mixen Lane" of Hardy's *The Mayor of Casterbridge*. "Vice ran freely in and out of the neighbourhood," which, he writes, bore a relation to the rest of Dorchester as "this mildewed leaf in the sturdy and flourishing ... plant". Less poetically, it was a district where, even at the time of Hardy's death, policemen would only patrol in pairs. Prostitution and houses of ill-fame abounded, as they did in the nearby, well-named Cuckolds Row, and children, as Florence found in her magistracy, were continually at risk. Part of this was due to the disreputable housing conditions. Since 1905, a local philanthropic Nonconformist, A. H. Edwards, had tried to save the souls and morals of the inhabitants through his undenominational Mill Street Mission. Now, with considerable insight and vision, he founded the Mill Street Housing Society, whose objects were registered under the Provident Societies Act, "to build houses or flats at the lowest possible rents" and to improve existing properties for families unable to afford council houses.

It was a bold and pioneering venture. England was entering on a period of slump, poverty and mass unemployment. In fact, one of the earliest minutes of the Society stated that employment would be given to unemployed builders and labourers.[4] It is a tribute to Florence's reputation in Dorchester that on 11 November 1931, the Committee of the Society unanimously agreed to ask her to act as Chairman, and on 1 June 1932, she laid the foundation stone of the first house. Her speech showed her real devotion and her common sense. She was evidently aware of the public distrust of investment in untried concerns at a time of national crisis, and pitched her appeal accordingly. She said "that healthy homes should help to keep children well and healthy", and then went on

> We hope to see many groups of houses like this, but that can only be if a large number join us and take shares and help to continue the work. I am told that the shares should be a really good and safe investment. There is another interest you may hope to have from the shares you take in this Society and that will be paid not in coin of this realm, but in coin of another realm where houses are not built by hands, but where there are many mansions.

It was appropriate and effective language for supporters of a Society which had grown out of the Mill Street Mission, and it was reported in the Mission bulletin. In November, the first show house was open for inspection, and the Society was well-found enough to borrow £2,250 from the Dorchester and Dorset Building Society to carry on the work, Florence being one of the guarantors, while the Society received a subsidy for each house from the Ministry of Health.

At every stage, Florence gave wise and helpful counsel, and showed great energy. Early on, applications from prospective tenants revealed "a large need", and she applied to the Ministry of Health for permission to build another six houses (ten in all), make up a roadway, and construct board fences. The needs of children were kept paramount in selecting tenants. Late in 1932, Florence personally wrote a letter[5] to *The Times*, outlining these aims and achievements. Headlined "Wise Spending", it put forward the example of the Society as illustration of a national need, "a practical illustration", as she said, of the policy not of retrenchment but of progressive investment. This publicity had the desired effect, and enquiries for details of investment in the Society followed, from as far afield as Birmingham, York, and Finchley.[6] The Committee was able to buy further land, "which will transform a scrap-heap, an eyesore and a public nuisance", while the annual report of the Medical Officer of Health confirmed that "houses of this sort"—three bedrooms and solidly built—"are so much needed".

In July 1933, this tale of success received its first set-back. As so often, this came from obstruction by local government. The Committee asked the Town Council to declare a slum clearance area, in order to obtain a subsidy for rebuilding under Section 29 of the Housing Act of 1930. The Housing Committee refused, as "houses mentioned could not be condemned as unfit for human habitation". There could be no subsidy, under the Act, without a slum clearance order. It was plain to Florence and her Committee though, whatever the local council said, that many houses were, in their present state, unfit. She now used her experience, her social contacts, and the influence she had acquired as the widow of a national figure to take up this local matter on a national basis. She wrote personally to the Minister of Health, Sir E. Hilton Young, inviting him to come and see Mill Street for himself, and to various members of Parliament about the need to change the terms of the Housing Act on Government subsidy. She published in *The Times* a further letter,[7] headed "Clearing the Slums". Written with practical directness, devoid of what she had always attempted as "literary style", it addressed itself to the general slowness of schemes for clearing the slums and rehousing, by giving an example of what her own Society had encountered, "in spite of all the energy and enthusiasm" shown by its members.

It is no wonder that in April of the following year, her Committee reported its grateful thanks, since

> by her pen she has dealt with matters far outside local affairs, but in the light of local experience has been able to point out very effectively the need for the amendment of section 29 of the Housing Act of 1930.

By the end of 1934, the Society owned and managed thirty-five houses, eighteen new and seventeen old, accommodating one hundred and fifty-five persons, consisting of one hundred adults and fifty-five children. Florence had represented the Society at the inaugural meeting in London of the National Federation of Housing Societies. The greatest encouragement came from the tenants themselves. Their gardens (for which the Society organized a competition) were "turning a wilderness into a place of beauty". Incidentally, whether she knew it or not, Florence was taking the most progressive path to assist the nation's recovery from the Depression. "The building boom", according to A. J. P. Taylor,[8] "was the outstanding cause for the recovery of the thirties." Unemployment, which had stood at two and a half million, was on the way down. Every local effort, such as hers in Mill Street, helped the main process.

Symbolically, this time of recovery and progress was marked by the celebrations of the Silver Jubilee of the reign of George V in 1935. The Mill Street Society greeted this with a children's playground, with seats for old people and mothers. It also in another way honoured its indefatigable Chairman. A row of newly-built houses, leading off King's Road, was to be known as Hardy Avenue. In the next year this road was made up and flowering trees planted, and on the bill being presented, Florence bought £350 of the Society's loan stock, which more than covered the cost. All through this year of 1936, she attended conferences and meetings in London and elsewhere, and acquired expert information and inspiration for the projects of the Society, which now could claim a total of twenty-two new houses and a communal wash-house, as well as many other public utility works. By spring 1937 the Society was flourishing as never before, and expressed its gratitude to her in appreciative sentences in the annual April report.

In all this, Florence on her part seems to have been carrying out the tradition of service to a local community instilled in her from her earliest years. Her father, who had just died in June 1936, had been, right up to his death, a director of the Enfield Building Society, which he had helped to found over fifty-five years before. Energetic to the last, his advice may even have assisted her with the Mill Street project. In many ways, she was now living the life from which her curious, self-sought destiny had diverted her.

16

"What Life Was"

"How quickly the years are slipping away," wrote Florence[1] sadly on 7 March 1937. Her sadness was more prophetic than she knew. In spite of what appeared an energetic, busy and useful life in so many local concerns, she herself was not to last the year. Since the "great and irreparable loss and sorrow" of her father's death[2] in the previous year, she had felt unable to bear up and resist either her own depression or her own insidious ill-health. The first week in May 1937 found her ill with new, disquieting symptoms, and "unable to write for some days". In alarm, when she could take a pen in hand again, she drew up a will, witnessed by the chauffeur, Dick Shipton, and her maid at Max Gate, Kathleen Bartlett.[3] By the first week in June, she was back at the scene of so many previous terrors, the Fitzroy House Nursing Home in London. Here she underwent an exploratory operation by Mr. Lindsey, surgeon of the London Hospital. The result was not favourable. Florence returned to Max Gate, where she remained under the care of two nurses and her sister Eva. The disease was terminal.

They moved her bed into the ground-floor drawing-room, which she had refurnished and relieved from "the Max Gate look". The brightly-coloured budgerigars, blue, green, and yellow, fluttered and chattered in her little conservatory that led from the room to the garden. Drugs kept at bay the worst of the pain, though they may also have been responsible for the many anxious codicils, witnessed by Kathleen Bartlett and the nurses, made to her will by the dying woman. Early in October, the local paper announced that she was too ill to see anyone. Her sister Marjorie joined Eva at the bedside. On 17 October, she died peacefully. She was only fifty-eight.

After cremation at Woking, attended by her sisters and some faithful literary friends, including the Tomlinsons, the ashes were buried in a casket at Stinsford, in the churchyard where Hardy had so often pointed out where she was to lie by him. Crowds stood in the pouring rain. The local tributes were intensely moving, none more so than those from Mill Street. The Society had sent a model of a house, covered in autumn leaves and red berries. Even more touching, the tenants had "spontaneously made a model of a small chair covered with flowers gathered from every garden".[4] Not only her own relatives attended, but Kate Hardy and even Gordon

16 The drawing-room at Max Gate, in which Florence died

Gifford's wife. Aristocracy was represented by Lady Ilchester and Lady Digby, Dorchester by the Mayor and representatives of every local concern to which Florence had lately belonged.

The national Press fell back on conventional platitudes.[5] Even in death, Florence found herself, ironically, "The Helpmate of Genius". As biographies of Hardy appeared, the references to her, though often complimentary, were brief and platitudinous, and gave no idea of her real character. She remained a shadowy background figure. The most garrulous of Hardy's biographers virtually ignored the hundreds of Florence's letters which have been preserved. He quoted half a page of brief extracts from them, and made a disapproving remark about some of the rest.[6] Except as author of Hardy's *Life*—which she was not—she is barely indexed in works on Hardy. If anything lingered, it was the vague identification of her with the second Mrs. Driffield in Maugham's *Cakes and Ale*.

Maugham indeed had denied, in a specially-written preface to the paperback edition of the book, that his characters had anything to do with Hardy. He produced the disingenuous argument that he had only met Hardy himself once, at a party given by Lady Jeune. In this, Maugham was telling a half-truth. His Driffield, in many points of character, is certainly nothing like Hardy; he is happy-go-lucky, sings comic songs to the banjo, does not pay his debts, and decamps under cover of darkness when creditors press. Nothing could be less like the careful master of Max Gate, even in his most youthful days. On the other hand, the book contains biting parodies which could only apply to the novels of Hardy, and to those of no other writer. His philosophic and sententious peasants discuss great themes in country pubs and in poetic language. The heavy insistence that they are nautical in profession and not agricultural underlines the satire. Hardy's inability to portray the upper classes, especially aristocratic ladies, is exposed in satire which even becomes surprisingly coarse. Yet it is the novels alone that point to Hardy as Driffield. Nothing could be less like Emma Hardy than Rosie, Driffield's first wife. She, in fact, did have an actual model, the lively daughter of the playwright Henry Arthur Jones, with whom Maugham had been deeply in love, and about whom he had long wanted to write.[7]

As for Florence, it will now be clear that in *character* she was almost totally unlike the second Mrs. Driffield. Where the fictional lady was managing, adroit, suave, calculating, Florence was nervously anxious, socially clumsy, uncertain, self-critical, impulsive, lacking in confidence. It was the *outward* circumstances of her life as Hardy's wife and widow which were satirized with such uncanny insight that she herself saw the likenesses, and shrank from doing anything that might "give colour" to them, after she had read the book. How did Maugham, who never visited Max Gate, gain his devastating half-knowledge? Some links in the process are still obscure; but once more, it would seem that Florence had too impulsively placed her confidence in unwise quarters. It seems likely that the channel, without perhaps himself being conscious of the process, was Siegfried Sassoon, through a friend he had brought to Max Gate before Hardy's death, and who is mentioned more than once in Florence's letters to him.[8]

Yet if Maugham's satire of Florence was external, superficial, and altogether by hearsay, his book's main satirical purpose had, unconsciously, much to do with the ideas by which she had tried to live her life. Her "eternal question of what life was", in Hardy's poetic phrase to her, was exposed by Maugham's chief plan in writing his book. For the book—apart from its tribute to the wayward and fascinating nature of Maugham's Rosie—is a trenchant criticism of the fashionable idea of the literary life, and, in particular, the absurdities of author-worship. True, the bitterest mockery is reserved for the character called Alroy Kear, so like Hugh Walpole—in spite of Maugham's strenuous denials—that when that popular and successful writer first read it he felt literally ill. Yet in his asides, prompted by the idea of the aged Driffield, Maugham, in the heart of the novel, satirized every item of belief that Florence herself had indeed expressed in her *Evening Standard* article on Hardy's seventieth birthday, a belief shared by her with the general reading public. He wrote:

> The cultured reader of these pages will remember the leading article in the *Literary Supplement* of *The Times* which appeared at the moment of Driffield's death. Taking the novels of Edward Driffield as his text, the author wrote what was very well described as a hymn to beauty. No one who read it could fail to be impressed by those swelling periods ...

Maugham then goes on to parody the kind of "funeral oration" in fact delivered, and put on a gramophone record, by Hardy's oldest surviving friend, Edmund Gosse. He added

> Roy Kear, when he was talking to me of Driffield, claimed that, whatever his faults, they were redeemed by the beauty that suffused his pages. Now I come to look back on our conversation, I think it was this remark that had most exasperated me.

Maugham then unleashed the full force of his satire on this kind of respectful worship.

> But of course what the critics wrote about Edward Driffield was eyewash. His outstanding merit was ... his longevity ... If, as I think, longevity is genius, few in our time have enjoyed it ... more ... When he was a young fellow in the sixties ... it was agreed that he had talent, but it never occurred to anyone that he was one of the glories of

English literature. He celebrated his seventieth birthday; an uneasiness passed over the world of letters, like a ruffling of the waters when on an Eastern sea a typhoon lurks in the distance, and it grew evident that there had lived among us all these years a great novelist and none of us had suspected it. There was a rush for Driffield's books in the various libraries and a hundred busy pens, in Bloomsbury, in Chelsea, and in other places where men of letters congregate, wrote appreciations, studies, essays, and works, short and chatty or long and intense, on his novels. These were reprinted, in complete editions, in select editions, at a shilling and three and six and five shillings and a guinea.

The worship of a false "Beauty" in English literature, the worship of "the Grand Old Man of English Letters"—Maugham's term for Driffield at the age of eighty—are at the heart of the deepest satire of Maugham's book. Yet these were, sincerely, the stuff of Florence's life. They were the background to everything with which she had passionately associated herself, the story-articles on the beauties of Nature in the *Enfield Observer*, Alfred Hyatt's painstaking little gift-book anthologies—including, of course, his actual selections from Hardy—the discussions of great authors in literary meetings at the Enfield Bycullah Athenaeum, to which she had contributed papers, the rather more ambitious literary evenings and conversaziones at the ladies' Lyceum Club. Above all, there was the "devotion" of her life to the idea of the great septuagenarian author, her acceptance of the influence he had acquired in the world of letters, to promote her own works, whose lack of talent was somehow suffused in the glow of his own achievement.

In all this, Florence appears as a victim of false, though popular, literary illusion. She subscribed to it with complete sincerity. She had no inkling how fragile these illusions were. Her marriage was ultimately based on them, and nearly all her subsequent life. It is true that she had chosen—so far as choice lay in her—a truly great writer, liable to satire and parody indeed, but of essential quality. It was her idea of the world of letters that injected falsity into her life, and was ultimately responsible for many of her bitterest unhappinesses.

It could even be argued that she found her real self, the idea of literature laid aside, after her husband's death. Her common sense, her kindness, her relief from anxieties, are surely shown in the decade of useful and far-sighted work for fellow human beings in Dorchester, for the poor and sick, and, like herself, the essentially lonely and troubled. A visitor[9] to Max Gate wrote "She was a dark, nervous woman, of an awkward carriage, who possessed an odd distinction of her own. As I stood by her side in that room emptied of its company I received a draught of romantic melancholy the strength of which I have never forgotten."

This cannot be a final verdict, even if a verdict of any sort were necessary or practicable. In one sense or another, and at whatever cost to herself, she preserved for us, in the last two decades of Hardy's life, the writing of imperishable poetry, over half Hardy's total output, and containing far and away his finest work in that medium. Would "what life was" have been the same if Florence Dugdale, and her nature, had never existed? Such questions are impossible to answer. What is certain is that her own unexplored history deserves telling, whether one regards her as a victim or as a gainer by its strange, human course.

Abbreviations Used in the Notes

DCM: Dorset County Museum.

DCRO: Dorset County Record Office.

MTH: *Materials for the Study of the Life, Times and Works of Thomas Hardy*, 72 monographs, St. Peter Port, Guernsey. Various dates from 1962.

ORFW: E. Hardy and F. B. Pinion (eds.), *One Rare Fair Woman: Thomas Hardy's Letters to Florence Henniker, 1893–1922*, London, 1972.

Purdy: R. L. Purdy, *Thomas Hardy, A Bibliographical Study*, Oxford, repr. 1968.

THYB: *Thomas Hardy Year Book*, St. Peter Port, Guernsey, Various dates.

TLS: *Times Literary Supplement*.

Notes

INTRODUCTION: *CAKES AND ALE*, pp. 1–5

1. Florence Hardy to Mrs. Cowley, 28 March 1928.
2. *Saturday Review of Literature*, 1 November 1930, New York.
3. TLS, 18 October 1930.
4. *Spectator*, 18 October 1930.
5. *Fortnightly Review*, 25 October 1930.
6. *Nation and Athenaeum*, 25 October 1930.
7. Published in two volumes, 1928 and 1930.
8. Florence Hardy to the Revd. H. G. B. Cowley, 20 October 1930.
9. Florence Hardy to Colonel Weber, 11 November 1930.
10. DCC.
11. Personal information, Dr. R. Bartellot.
12. Florence Hardy to Sydney Cockerell, 10 November 1916.
13. Florence Hardy to Siegfried Sassoon, 12 May 1928.
14. Plans kindly shown by the present tenants, Mr. and Mrs. Jesty, who have transformed the old, gloomy Max Gate.
15. Florence Hardy to Rebekah Owen, 15 May 1916.
16. Photograph of drawing-room, Max Gate, DCM.
17. Florence Hardy to Rebekah Owen, 4 August 1920.
18. V. Meynell (ed.), *Friends of a Lifetime*, 304.
19. Florence Hardy to Alda, Lady Hoare, 7 April 1914.
20. Florence Hardy to Louisa Yearsley, 19 June 1921.
21. Florence Hardy to Louisa Yearsley, 1 June 1920.
22. Florence Hardy to Rebekah Owen, 1 March 1916.
23. Florence Hardy to Rebekah Owen, 24 October 1915.
24. Florence Hardy to Siegfried Sassoon, 5 November 1930.

1: "QUIET, HUMBLE AND OBEDIENT", pp. 9–15

1. *Parliamentary Papers*, 1873, XXIV, 25–6.
2. *1861 Census*, Lansdown Street, St. Paul's Parish, Portsea. An inn at Poole harbour was called *The Portsmouth Hoy.*
3. *Enfield Observer*, 15 February 1929.
4. St. Andrew's Church, Enfield, *Register of Baptisms.*
5. St. Andrew's Infants' School Log-Book, 1884–6.
6. St. Andrew's Girls' School Log-Book, October 1891.
7. Diocesan Inspector's Report, April 1888.
8. MTH, No. 14, 14–15.
9. Florence Hardy to Rebekah Owen, 26 October 1916.
10. *Enfield Observer*, 5 September 1936.
11. *Enfield Observer*, 20 August 1970.
12. Personal information from the sister of the boy, Ivor Johns.
13. D. Pam, *The New Enfield*, A Jubilee History, 15.
14. Kelly, *Directory of Herts, Essex and Middlesex*, 1908, Vol. II, 112–29.
15. *Enfield Observer*, 15 February 1929.
16. *Thomas Hardy Society Review*, 1978, 100.
17. *Enfield Observer*, classified advertisements, 1890.
18. Personal information, Miss G. Barker.
19. Florence Hardy to Rebekah Owen, 26 November 1915.
20. Florence Hardy to Rebekah Owen, 1 October 1915.
21. St. Andrew's Girls' School Log-Book, 1895.

22. Postcard, showing ward, from Eva Dugdale, 30 December 1909. Kate Hardy's postcard collection.
23. Florence Hardy to Rebekah Owen, 22 March 1916 and n.d. March 1917.
24. Foundation stone inscription.
25. St Andrew's Girls' School Log-Book, 1895–7.
26. P. H. J. H. Gosden (ed.), *How They Were Taught*, 206–14.
27. St. Andrew's Girls' School Log-Book, 9 June 1894.
28. St. Andrew's Girls' School Log-Book, 8 June 1896.
29. *Enfield Observer*, 26 June 1896.
30. ibid.

2: "THE DRUDGERY OF TEACHING", pp. 16–23

1. St. Andrew's Boys' School Log-Book, 22 December 1897.
2. St. Andrew's Boys' School Log-Book, 23 October 1905.
3. Personal information, Mr. P. A. Glennie, present headmaster of St. Andrew's Junior Mixed School.
4. *Enfield Observer*, 15 February 1929.
5. St. Andrew's Boys' School Log-Book, 16 February 1905.
6. St. Andrew's Boys' School Log-Book, n.d. May 1912.
7. M. Arnold (H.M.I.), General Report for 1863.
8. *Cornhill Magazine*, June 1908, "The Apotheosis of the Minx".
9. St. Andrew's Boys' School Log-Book, 31 March 1905.
10. Personal information, Mr. J. Westaway, M.B.E.
11. Postcard in the possession of Mr. Louis Davis. Personal information recorded and kindly made available by Dr. Graham Handley.
12. St. Andrew's Boys' School Log-Book, 31 March 1905.
13. St. Andrew's Boys' School Log-Book, n.d. June 1910.
14. *Alumni Cantabrigiensis*.
15. Personal information, Ms. S. Collicott, who kindly made her research on the Enfield School Board available.
16. Florence Hardy to Louisa Yearsley, 10 November 1918.
17. Florence Hardy to Rebekah Owen, 17 July 1915.
18. Florence Hardy's Diary, 26 December 1927.
19. J. S. MacClure (ed.), *Educational Documents 1810–1963*, 73.
20. St. Andrew's Boys' School Log-Book, 5 September 1906.
21. St. Andrew's Boys' School Log-Book, n.d. January 1908.
22. Florence Dugdale to Emma Hardy, n.d. November 1910.
23. St. Andrew's Boys' School Log-Book, 27 January 1899.
24. St. Andrew's Boys' School Log-Book, 1 July 1904.
25. Personal information, Mr. Louis Davis.
26. *Cornhill Magazine*, June 1908, "The Apotheosis of the Minx".
27. MTH, No. 19, Joyce Scudamore.
28. *The Times*, 15 October 1937.

3: "I LOVE WRITING", pp. 24–29

1. Florence Hardy to Alda, Lady Hoare, 26 July 1914.
2. Florence Hardy to Alda, Lady Hoare, 10 October 1914.
3. Florence Hardy to Louisa Yearsley, 10 November 1918.
4. Florence Hardy to Alda, Lady Hoare, 27 March 1915.
5. *Parliamentary Papers*, 1884–5, XXIII, 460.
6. *Enfield Observer*, 22 November 1901.
7. *Enfield Observer*, 15 December 1911.
8. Florence Hardy to Rebekah Owen, 1 December 1914.
9. Personal information recorded by Dr. Graham Handley.
10. *Enfield Observer*, 6 January 1903.

11. *Enfield Observer*, 31 July 1903.
12. A. H. Hyatt, *From a Middlesex Garden*, 109.
13. Edward Clodd, Diary, 30 June 1910.
14. *Enfield Observer*, 15 December 1911.
15. Thomas Hardy to Edward Clodd, 22 July 1909.
16. Note by Macmillan office on Florence Dugdale's visiting card, 5 July 1907. Macmillan Archive, British Library.
17. Florence Hardy to Rebekah Owen, 1 December 1914.
18. Florence Hardy to Alda, Lady Hoare, 24 April 1920.
19. C. Weber, *Hardy of Wessex*, 218–19.
20. Dates kindly given by Professor Michael Millgate, co-editor of *The Collected Letters of Thomas Hardy*.
21. Thomas Hardy to Frederick Macmillan, 11 May 1906, British Library.
22. A. H. Hyatt (ed.), *The Pocket Thomas Hardy*, 1906.
23. British Museum Secretariat.

4: "A SCRIBBLING WOMAN", pp. 30–37

1. Edward Clodd to Clement Shorter, 16 February 1908.
2. Florence Hardy to Sydney Cockerell, 18 February 1918.
3. Dates kindly given by Professor Michael Millgate.
4. Florence Hardy to Alda, Lady Hoare, 9 April 1914.
5. Florence Hardy to Marie Stopes, 14 September 1923.
6. Florence Hardy to Rebekah Owen, 26 October 1916.
7. Thomas Hardy to Frederick Macmillan, 8 July 1907, British Library.
8. Macmillan Archive, British Library.
9. Reginald Smith to Thomas Hardy, 23 September 1907, DCM.
10. *Cornhill Magazine*, June 1908.
11. Thomas Hardy to Edward Clodd, 22 July 1909.
12. St. Andrew's Boys' School Log-Book, 17 March 1908.
13. Thomas Hardy to Emma Hardy, 25 May 1908, DCM.
14. A. H. Hyatt, *A Guide to Enfield and its Neighbourhood*, 1908.
15. *The Sphere*, 30 May 1908.
16. St Andrew's Boys' School Log-Book, 13 May 1908.
17. Florence Hardy to Rebekah Owen, 3 November 1915.
18. Florence Hardy to Rebekah Owen, 3 November 1916.
19. Florence Hardy to Rebekah Owen, 1 March 1916.
20. *The Sphere*, 12 and 19 September 1908.
21. Florence Hardy to Rebekah Owen, 26 August 1915.
22. *The Sphere*, 27 June 1908.
23. *The Sphere*, 1 August 1908.
24. *The Sphere*, 5 September 1908.
25. *The Sphere*, 17 October 1908.
26. *The Sphere*, 2 January 1909.
27. *The Sphere*, 28 November 1908.
28. Florence Hardy to Rebekah Owen, 30 January 1916.
29. Florence Hardy to Rebekah Owen, 29 July 1917.
30. Florence Hardy to Rebekah Owen, 1 March 1916.
31. Florence Hardy to Rebekah Owen, 16 February 1916.
32. Florence Hardy to Alda, Lady Hoare, 19 December 1914.
33. Thomas Hardy to Edward Clodd, 22 July 1909.

5: "DEAR, KIND FRIENDS", pp. 38–45

1. Florence Dugdale to Edward Clodd, 7 March 1913.
2. Florence Hardy to Rebekah Owen, 1 March 1916.
3. Florence Hardy to Rebekah Owen, 3 December 1915.
4. Florence Dugdale to Emma Hardy, 1 December 1910.

5. *The Sphere*, 16 January 1909.
6. C. Shorter, *An Autobiography*, 138–43.
7. Kate Hardy's postcard collection.
8. Compare Florence's correspondence with Mrs. Hardy in 1910 or with the Hon. Mrs. Henniker in 1911.
9. Florence Hardy to Rebekah Owen, 20 October 1915.
10. *The Irish Times*, 15 October 1910, 12.
11. J. Hone, *George Moore*, 232.
12. Personal information, Sir Thornley Stoker's great-niece.
13. Florence Dugdale to Mrs. Hardy, n.d. November 1910.
14. *British Medical Journal*, 15 June 1912.
15. O. St.J. Gogarty, *It Isn't the Time of Year at All*, 34–6.
16. G. Moore, *Hail and Farewell*, II, 115–16.
17. *The Irish Times*, 15 October 1910, 12.
18. Florence Dugdale to Emma Hardy, 11 December 1910.
19. Author, later Mrs. G. T. Huntington.
20. Florence Hardy to Rebekah Owen, 17 December 1916.
21. J. Hone, *George Moore*, 265.
22. Florence Hardy to Rebekah Owen, 1 March 1916.
23. Florence Hardy to Rebekah Owen, 1 June 1914.
24. O. St.J. Gogarty, *It Isn't the Time of Year at All*, 35–6.
25. O. St.J. Gogarty, *As I Was Going Down Sackville Street*, 292–3.
26. Florence Dugdale to Emma Hardy, 18 June 1910.
27. Florence Hardy to Rebekah Owen, 22 January 1916.
28. Lady C. Asquith, *Portrait of Barrie*, 108 and 171.

6: "TIMES NOT EASY", pp. 46–54

1. *The Lyceum*—monthly magazine of the Lyceum Club.
2. Florence Dugdale to Edward Clodd, 11 November 1910.
3. N. Syrett, *The Sheltering Tree*, 194.
4. Personal recollections, Kathleen Gibberd.
5. Florence Hardy to Rebekah Owen, 1 March 1916.
6. Edward Clodd, Diary, 5 July 1909.
7. Thomas Hardy to Edward Clodd, 22 July 1909.
8. Thomas Hardy to Edward Clodd, 13 July 1909.
9. Edward Clodd, Diary, 14 July 1909.
10. Edward Clodd to Clement Shorter, 17 August 1909.
11. Edward Clodd, Diary, 16 August 1909.
12. Edward Clodd to Clement Shorter, 17 August 1909.
13. Edward Clodd, Diary, 20 August 1909.
14. Edward Clodd to Clement Shorter, 27 August 1909.
15. Edward Clodd, *Memories*, 84–5.
16. Edward Clodd, Diary, 30 October 1909.
17. Florence Dugdale to Edward Clodd, 30 January 1913.
18. Thomas Hardy, postcards to Kate Hardy, 14 April 1911, 11 May 1912, 9 July 1912.
19. Florence Dugdale to Edward Clodd, 24 February 1911.
20. E. M. Richardson, *St. Katharine's College Magazine*, "Recollections of Thomas Hardy, O.M."
21. Thomas Hardy to Edward Clodd, 17 June 1910.
22. *Evening Standard and St. James's Gazette*, 2 June 1910, 3.
23. Thomas Hardy to Edward Clodd, 17 June 1910.
24. Edward Clodd, Diary, 30 June 1910.
25. Thomas Hardy to Edward Clodd, 17 June 1910.
26. MTH, No. 54.
27. Florence Dugdale to Emma Hardy, 18 June 1910.
28. Florence Dugdale to Emma Hardy, 3 July 1910.
29. Edward Clodd, Diary, 23 June 1910.

7: "MUTE MINISTRATIONS", pp. 55–64

1. Edward Clodd, Diary, 8 August 1910.
2. Florence Dugdale to Edward Clodd, 17 March 1913 and photographs, DCM.
3. Florence Dugdale to Edward Clodd, 11 and 19 November 1910.
4. Florence Dugdale to Emma Hardy, n.d. 1910.
5. Florence Dugdale to Emma Hardy, n.d. 1910.
6. Florence Dugdale to Emma Hardy, 3 July 1910.
7. Florence Dugdale to Emma Hardy, 26 August 1910.
8. Florence Dugdale to Emma Hardy, 30 September 1910.
9. Edward Clodd, Diary, 27 April 1913.
10. Florence Dugdale to Emma Hardy, 22 November 1910.
11. Florence Dugdale to Emma Hardy, n.d. October 1910.
12. Florence Hardy to Rebekah Owen, 18 January 1916.
13. Edward Clodd, Diary, 25 May 1911.
14. Florence Dugdale to Edward Clodd, 19 November 1910.
15. Florence Dugdale to Edward Clodd, 11 November 1910.
16. Florence Dugdale to Edward Clodd, 11 November 1910.
17. Dated and dedicated drawing, DCM.
18. Florence Dugdale to Edward Clodd, 30 June 1913.
19. Edward Clodd, Diary, 13 July 1913.
20. Florence Dugdale to Mary Hardy, 3 November 1910, to Kate Hardy, 20 October 1910.
21. Emma Hardy to London Society for Women's Suffrage, 21, 22 and 23 June 1910.
22. Emma Hardy to London Society for Women's Suffrage, 18 May 1911. Fawcett Society, copies kindly supplied by Dr. Graham Handley.
23. Florence Dugdale to Emma Hardy, n.d. November 1910.
24. Florence Hardy to Edward Clodd, 19 November 1910.
25. Florence Dugdale to Emma Hardy, 11 December 1910.
26. *The Times*, 14 November 1910.
27. Florence Hardy to Rebekah Owen, n.d. 1919.
28. ORFW, 147.
29. ORFW, 143.
30. Florence Hardy to Louisa Yearsley, 6 January 1923.
31. R. Blaythwaite, *The Woman at Home*, "The Hon. Mrs. Arthur Henniker."
32. Florence Hardy to Rebekah Owen, 15 December 1914.
33. Florence Dugdale to Edward Clodd, 24 February 1911.
34. Thomas Hardy to Edward Clodd, 9 March 1911.
35. Thomas Hardy to Edward Clodd, 3 October 1911.
36. Florence Dugdale to Mary Hardy, 9 August 1911.
37. *Later Life*, typescript, 504, DCM.
38. ORFW.
39. Death certificate, Alfred Henry Hyatt, 9 December 1911, General Registry.
40. Florence Dugdale to Edward Clodd, 11 December 1911.
41. Florence Hardy to Rebekah Owen, 1 December 1914.

8: "FROM YOUTH TO DREARY MIDDLE-AGE", pp. 65–73

1. ORFW, 147.
2. ORFW, 162–3.
3. Florence Hardy to Rebekah Owen, 30 December 1915.
4. Florence Dugdale to Edward Clodd, 7 March 1913.
5. *British Medical Journal*, 15 June 1912.
6. Will of Sir Thornley Stoker Bt., General Registry.
7. Personal information, Bram Stoker's grand-daughter.
8. Florence Hardy to Rebekah Owen, 22 March 1916.
9. Personal information, Mr. Louis Davis.
10. Published H. Frowde, Oxford University Press and Hodder, 1912.
11. E. Blunden, *Thomas Hardy*, 106 and 109.
12. ORFW, 155.

13. THYB, No. 4.
14. Florence Hardy to Sydney Cockerell, 26 November 1922.
15. ORFW, 155.
16. Florence Dugdale to Edward Clodd, 16 January 1913.
17. Florence Dugdale to Edward Clodd, 16 January 1913.
18. Florence Dugdale to Edward Clodd, 30 January 1913.
19. Information kindly supplied by James Gibson.
20. Personal information, Miss E. M. Lane.
21. Florence Dugdale to Edward Clodd, 7 March 1913.
22. Edward Clodd, Diary, 25 April 1913.
23. Florence Dugdale to Edward Clodd, 7 March 1913.
24. Florence Dugdale to Edward Clodd, 30 January 1913.
25. Thomas Hardy to Edward Clodd, 18 April 1913.
26. Florence Dugdale to Edward Clodd, 30 June 1913.
27. Florence Dugdale to Edward Clodd, 30 January 1913.
28. Edward Clodd, Diary, 11–13 July 1913.
29. Florence Dugdale to Edward Clodd, 21 August 1913.
30. ORFW, 160.
31. Florence Hardy to Alda, Lady Hoare, 22 July 1914.
32. MTH, No. 59.
33. Florence Hardy to Rebekah Owen, 30 December 1915.
34. ORFW, xxiii.
35. Florence Hardy to Rebekah Owen, 22 March 1916.
36. Florence Hardy to Rebekah Owen, 17 December 1915.
37. ORFW, 158.
38. Florence Dugdale to Edward Clodd, 1 January 1914.
39. Thomas Hardy to Alda, Lady Hoare, 13 February 1914.
40. Florence Hardy to Rebekah Owen, 30 December 1915.
41. Information supplied by Dr. Graham Handley.
42. ORFW, 160.
43. Florence Hardy to Sydney Cockerell, 10 February 1917.
44. Florence Hardy to Rebekah Owen, 20 September 1915.
45. St. Andrew's Boys' School Log-Book, 10 February 1914.

9: "IF MY NAME WERE GIFFORD", pp. 77–83

1. Florence Hardy to Edward Clodd, 12 February 1914.
2. Florence Hardy to Edward Clodd, 27 February 1914.
3. Florence Hardy to Alda, Lady Hoare, 27 May 1914.
4. Information given by Denys Kay-Robinson.
5. Florence Hardy to Alda, Lady Hoare, 15 and 22 July, 1914.
6. Florence Hardy to Alda, Lady Hoare, 6 December 1914.
7. Edward Clodd, Diary.
8. Kate Hardy's Diary.
9. Florence Hardy to Alda, Lady Hoare, 6 August 1915.
10. Florence Hardy to Edward Clodd, 28 November 1915.
11. Florence Hardy to Rebekah Owen, 16 February 1916.
12. Florence Hardy to Rebekah Owen, 5 May and 25 August 1916.
13. Obituary, *Enfield Observer*.
14. Florence Hardy to Rebekah Owen, 4 March 1917 and Kate Hardy's Diary.
15. Florence Hardy to Rebekah Owen, 4 March 1917.
16. Florence Hardy to Alda, Lady Hoare, 26 July 1914.
17. Florence Hardy to Rebekah Owen, 3 December 1916.

10: "A TREMENDOUS JOB IN HAND", pp. 84–90

1. Florence Hardy to Alda, Lady Hoare, 5 September 1916.
2. Purdy, 349–50.

3. Thomas Hardy to Clement Shorter, 15 March 1916.
4. Florence Hardy to Rebekah Owen, 28 August 1917.
5. Macmillan Archive, British Library.
6. Florence Hardy to Louisa Yearsley, 17 June 1917.
7. Florence Hardy to Rebekah Owen, 25 May 1920.

11: "REGARDED AND TREATED AS HOSTESS", pp. 91–98

1. *Letters*, 71.
2. Florence Hardy to Rebekah Owen, 4 March 1917.
3. Florence Hardy to Rebekah Owen, 5 June 1916.
4. Florence Hardy to Alda, Lady Hoare, 9 December 1914.
5. Florence Hardy to Alda, Lady Hoare, 5 September 1916.
6. Florence Hardy to Alda, Lady Hoare, 31 December 1914.
7. Florence Hardy to Louisa Yearsley, May 1917.
8. Florence Hardy to Louisa Yearsley, 10 November 1918.
9. Gordon N. Ray, *H. G. Wells and Rebecca West*, 94–5.
10. Florence Hardy to Louisa Yearsley, 27 February 1920.
11. Florence Hardy to Louisa Yearsley, 25 March 1925.
12. Florence Hardy to Siegfried Sassoon, 27 October 1927.
13. Florence Hardy to Louisa Yearsley, 10 November 1918.
14. Letter from Mrs. M. Wilson, *Sunday Times*, 3 March 1978. When the vicar saw the Hardys arrive, he always changed the hymn to Hardy's favourite, "Lead, kindly Light".

12: "THINGS THAT ONE CANNOT WRITE ABOUT", pp. 99–106

1. Florence Hardy to Louisa Yearsley, 23 February 1923.
2. Florence Hardy to Louisa Yearsley, 20 June 1924.
3. Florence Hardy to Louisa Yearsley, 18 January 1920.
4. MTH, No. 59.
5. Florence Hardy to Rebekah Owen, 22 January 1916.
6. Florence Hardy to Louisa Yearsley, 30 December 1920.
7. V. Meynell (ed.), *Friends of a Lifetime*, 357.
8. Personal information, Mrs. G. Bugler.
9. Macmillan Archive, British Library.
10. Florence Hardy to Rebekah Owen, 16 February 1925.
11. V. Meynell (ed.), *Letters of J. M. Barrie*, 149.
12. Florence Hardy to Siegfried Sassoon, 17 December 1929.
13. Florence Hardy's Diary, DCM.

13: "SO FUTILE AND HOPELESS", pp. 107–112

1. MTH, No. 59.
2. MS. of *Life*, etc. Mrs. Hardy's copy, DCM.
3. Florence Hardy to Louisa Yearsley, n.d. 1924.
4. Florence Hardy to Siegfried Sassoon, 20 May 1928.
5. Florence Hardy to Siegfried Sassoon, 12 May 1928.
6. Florence Hardy to Siegfried Sassoon, 24 February 1928.
7. Florence Hardy to Siegfried Sassoon, 13 March 1928.
8. Florence Hardy to Siegfried Sassoon, 17 December 1929.
9. Florence Hardy to Siegfried Sassoon, 5 November 1930.
10. V. Meynell (ed.), *The Best of Friends*, 45.
11. MTH, No. 12.

14: "TIME AND HER FRIENDS", pp. 113–121

1. V. Meynell (ed.), *Friends of a Lifetime*, 368.
2. DCRO.
3. MTH, No. 59.
4. ORFW, 147.
5. Florence Hardy to Paul Lemperly, 26 October 1928.
6. Florence Hardy to Paul Lemperly, 25 February 1934.
7. MTH, No. 59.
8. MTH, No. 59.
9. Florence Hardy to Rebekah Owen, 23 June 1915.
10. DCM. All subsequent quotations from the typescripts in DCM under Barrie.
11. MTH, No. 59.
12. DCM.
13. C. Asquith, *Portrait of Barrie*, 56–7.
14. J. Dunbar, *J. M. Barrie*, 203–4.
15. C. Asquith, *Portrait of Barrie*, 171.
16. W. Blunt, *Cockerell*, 223.
17. Florence Hardy to Siegfried Sassoon, 8 November 1933.
18. Personal communication, Peter Coxon, from his forthcoming article in the THYB.
19. DCM.
20. Florence Hardy to Paul Lemperly, 17 March 1935.
21. Florence Hardy to Paul Lemperly, 7 April 1935.

15: "COIN OF ANOTHER REALM", pp. 122–128

1. *Dorset County Hospital Annual Reports*.
2. *Dorset County Hospital Annual Reports*.
3. *Borough of Dorchester Petty Sessions Minute Book*, 1933–6.
4. Mill Street Housing Society Ltd., Minutes.
5. *The Times*, 1 December 1932.
6. Mill Street Housing Society Ltd., Minutes.
7. *The Times*, 30 August 1933.
8. A. J. P. Taylor, *English History 1914–1945*, 345.

16: "WHAT LIFE WAS", pp. 129–134

1. Florence Hardy to Paul Lemperly, 7 March 1937.
2. Florence Hardy to Paul Lemperly, 27 July 1936.
3. MTH, No. 36.
4. Mill Street Housing Society Ltd., Minutes.
5. *The Times*, 18 October 1937.
6. C. J. Weber, *Hardy and the Lady from Madison Square*.
7. Robert L. Calder, *W. Somerset Maugham and the Quest for Freedom*, Appendix A.
8. Florence Hardy to Siegfried Sassoon, 15 November 1928 and 17 December 1929.
9. Llewellyn Powys, "Thomas Hardy", *The Virginian Quarterly Review* No. 15 (Winter 1939), 430.

Short List of Printed Sources

(Manuscript and typescript sources are listed in Acknowledgements.)

A.BOOKS, ETC.

Alumni Cantabrigiensis.

Asquith, C., *Portrait of Barrie*, London, 1954.

Blunden, E., *Thomas Hardy*, London, 1962.

Blunt, W., *Cockerell*, London, 1964.

Calder, R. L., *W. Somerset Maugham and the Quest for Freedom*, London, 1972.

Clodd, E., *Memories*, London, 1916.

Dunbar, J., *J. M. Barrie*, London, 1970.

Gittings, R., *Young Thomas Hardy*, London, 1975.

 The Older Hardy, London, 1978.

Gosden, P. H. J. H. (ed.), *How They Were Taught*, Oxford, 1969.

Hone, J., *George Moore*, London, 1936.

Hyatt, A. H., *From A Middlesex Garden*, London, 1901.

 (ed.), *The Pocket Thomas Hardy*, London, 1906.

 A Guide to Enfield and its Neighbourhood, London, 1908.

MacClure, J. S. (ed.) *Educational Documents 1810–1963*, London, 1965.

Meynell, V., (ed.), *Friends of a Lifetime: Letters to Sydney Cockerell*, London, 1940.

 Letters of J. M. Barrie, London, 1942.

Moore, G., *Hail and Farewell*, London, 2nd. edition, 1925.

Pam, D., *The New Enfield*.

Parliamentary Papers, Reports of H.M. Inspectors of Schools, 1873, 1884–5.

Purdy, R. L., *Thomas Hardy: A Bibliographical Study*, Oxford, 1954, repr. 1968.

Ray, Gordon N., *H. G. Wells and Rebecca West*, London, 1974.

Shorter, C., *An Autobiography*, privately printed, 1927.

Syrett, N., *The Sheltering Tree*, London, 1939.

Taylor, A. J. P., *English History, 1914–1945*, Oxford, 1965.

Weber, C. J., *Hardy and the Lady From Madison Square*, Waterville, Maine, 1952.

 Hardy of Wessex, London, 1940: rev. and repr., 1965.

B. MAGAZINES, NEWSPAPERS, PERIODICALS

The local Enfield paper which changed its name at various times during Florence's lifetime
 is listed under *Enfield Observer*.

British Medical Journal

Cornhill Magazine

Dorset County Chronicle

Enfield Observer

Evening Standard and St. James's Gazette

Fortnightly Review

Irish Times

Nation and Athenaeum

Saturday Review of Literature

Spectator

The Sphere

Sunday Times

The Times

Times Literary Supplement

Index

Florence Hardy is referred to as F.H. and Thomas Hardy as T.H.

Ainley, Henry, 79
Arnold, Matthew, 9, 15, 18
Asquith, Lady Cynthia, 115, 118
—Herbert Henry, 1st Earl of Oxford and Asquith, 118
Austen, Jane, 13

Barrie, Sir James, and T.H.'s Abbey burial, 105, 107; and T.H.'s memorial, 109; and biography of T.H., 110, 119; and F.H., 114, 115, 116–20; behaviour to women, 118; correspondence with F.H., 120, 121
Bartlett, Kathleen, 129
Beerbohm, Sir Max, 114
Benson, E.F., 31
Birrell, Augustine, 43
Blanche, Jacques-Emile, 54
Blunden, Edmund, 96
Boswell, James, 88
Boughton, Rutland, 104
Brennecke, Ernest, 96
Broughton, Rhoda, 13
Browning, Robert, 106
Bugler, Gertrude, 101–3, 114
Burdett, Osbert, 111
Burnett, Frances Hodgson, 66

Caine, Sir Hall, 51
Churchill, Sir Winston, 35, 77
—Lady, 35, 77
Clodd, Edward, 101; history and personality, 47; and F.H., 49, 81–2; F.H. and T.H. his guests, 49–51, 63; his kindness, 51, 53; his memoirs, 51, 81–2, 88; F.H.'s article on, 53, 93; F.H.'s confidant, 54, 55, 56, 57, 61, 64, 68, 69, 72, 79; to lecture at Enfield, 68; on death of Emma Hardy, 68; and compromising situation of F.H., 69–70; on T.H.'s relations, 70; stays with Hardys, 77, 80; second marriage, 79–80; deception over Hardys' visits to, 88; and T.H.'s Life, 108
—Mrs. Edward, 93
Cockerell, Sir Sidney, 102, 103, 105; F.H. writes to, 77; and limited edition of T.H.'s poems, 87; and T.H.'s funeral, 107; T.H.'s trustee, 109; and T.H.'s memorial, 109;

and F.H., 109, 111, 119; Sassoon and, 110; malicious gossip about Barrie and F.H., 119–20
Corelli, Marie, 46
Cornhill Magazine, 32, 33, 63, 88, 90
Crewe, Robert Crewe Milnes, Marquess of, 61

Daily Mail, 53
Dawson, Father Thomas, 65
Deeping, Warwick, 46
de la Mare, Walter, 96, 105
D'Erlanger, Baron Frederic, 49
Detmold, E. J., 63, 84
Dew, Miss, 14
Dickens, Charles, 34, 61
Dorset County Museum, 121
Dorset General Hospital, 122–3
Dublin, Ely House, 38, 39–41, 60
Dugdale, Constance, F.H.'s sister, 10, 14, 80, 83
—Edward, F.H.'s father, 86; family background and early history, 9–10; house owner, 11; public figure, 11–12; and F.H., 12, 16, 21, 22, 23; on causes of truancy, 16; health, 18, 82; disciplinarian, 18, 73; end of F.H.'s teaching career, 34; at Hardy's wedding, 73; life span, 82; death of, 128, 129
—Emily, née Hibbs, F.H.'s grandmother, 9
—Emma, née Taylor, F.H.'s mother, 72; early history, 10; makes a happy home, 11; her kindness and generosity, 16, 18; physical and mental health, 22, 38, 56, 82
—Ethel, F.H.'s sister, 10, 14, 15, 51–2
—Eva, F.H.'s sister, 82; birth, 10; Stoker recommends, 42–3; and F.H., 93, 129; and death of T.H., 116; nurses T.H., 116; F.H.'s bequest to, 120–21
—Florence Emily, see Hardy, Florence Emily
—Margaret, F.H.'s sister, birth, 10; marriage and honeymoon, 14, 82–3; F.H. sends her to college, 66; at Hardy's wedding, 73; stays with Hardys, 80, 97; pregnant, 93; her son, 97; and death of F.H., 129
—William, F.H.'s grandfather, 9
du Maurier, George, 91

education, Arnold on, 9, 18; Education Act of 1870, 9, 10; in late nineteenth century, 10–11; fees, 13; teacher training, 13–14; pupil–teachers, 14–15; curriculum, 15, 18–19; teaching apprenticeship, 16; National Schools, 19, 21; teachers and clergy, 22

Edwards, A. H., 125

Enfield, its development in nineteenth century, 12; becomes a local authority, 21; literary societies, 24, 46, 68, 133; F.H. on, 59; F.H. spends Christmas at, 60; T.H. visits Dugdales at, 72

Enfield Observer, 26, 27, 32, 46, 133

Ervine, St. John, 99

Evening Standard, 52–3, 93, 132

Farnol, Jeffrey, 46

Foster, E. M., 96

Garnett, Constance, 38–9

Garrick, David, 115

George, Frank, 81

Gibberd, Alan, 47

—Kathleen, 47

—Vernon, 46–7

Gifford, Gordon, 83, 92, 104, 108

—Mrs. Gordon, 116, 131

—Lilian, F.H. on, 68, 70–71, 80, 92; intends to make her home with T.H., 70; T.H. forced to choose between F.H. and, 72

Gogarty, St. John, 40, 42, 43

Gosse, Edmund, 120, 132

Granville-Barker, Harley, 79

Graves, Robert, 96, 110

Hanbury, Mrs., 80–81, 100, 114

Hardy, Emma Lavinia, T.H.'s first wife, 72; subject of "The Ivy Wife", 29; F.H.'s belief about, 45; and May Sinclair, 46; and Clodd, 47; to London for *Tess*, 49; death of, 50–51, 67; relationship with F.H., 53–4, 55, 56, 59; relationship with T.H., 55, 122; her kindness, 56; a cat lover, 56, 67, 104; aspiring author, 56; Protestant, 56, 59–60, 92; attitude to women's suffrage, 59; ill-health, 63; holiday with F.H., 63–4; her diaries, 69; T.H.'s obsession with her after her death, 69, 71, 77–8, 108; family quarrel, 70; her frugality, 78; unfavourable attitudes to, 91–2; and *Life of* T.H., 108; and attempted deception about relationship between F.H. and, 108; F.H. destroys her effects, 109

—Works: *The Inspirer* 56; *The Maid on the Shore*, 56; *Some Recollections*, 57

—Florence Emily, née Dugdale (*for relationship with T.H. see* Hardy, Thomas), attitude to visitors, 3; and *Cakes and Ale*, 3–7, 131–3; upbringing, 4; and the Hardy memorial at Stinsford, 4–5; appearance,

6–7, 30; birth, 10; education, 10–11, 13; on her childhood, 13; her interest in literature, 13, 19; health, 14, 15, 22–3, 33, 63, 80, 86, 87, 93, 99–100, 102, 103, 122, 123, 129; attitude to religion, 21, 30, 65, 105, 108; her paper on *Idylls of the King*, 25; range of her reading, 27; and Hyatt, 25–8, 36, 51, 60, 64, 65; and *The Pocket Thomas Hardy*, 29; interests, 27, 35–6, 52; attitude to sex, 31, 69; attitude to women, 36, 42, 104; Lady Stoker's companion, 39–40, 43; influence of life at Ely House on, 40–42, 45; attitude to politics, 42; member of Lyceum Club, 46; gives paper on T.H., 46; to *Tess* with Clodd, 49; Clodd's guest with T.H. at Aldeburgh, 49–51, 63; is lent Baker Street flat, 51–3; and Emma Hardy, 53–4, 55, 56–7, 59, 63–4, 69, 90; and Florence Henniker, 60–61; financial affairs, 66, 67, 71, 122; shadow of Emma, 63, 69, 73, 77–8, 79, 83, 86, 104, 109; mistress of Max Gate, 77, housekeeping, 78–9, 93, 97, 99; attitude to 1914 War, 79; childless, 81, 104; and Clodd's memoirs, 81–2; resentful of Gifford family, 83, 87, 92, 107; as a correspondent, 92; sycophant, 92–3; and Louisa Yearsley, 93; hostess, 95–7; an unfortunate photograph, 96; keeps hens, 96, 97; and Gertrude Bugler, 101, 102–3, 114; destroys Emma's effects, 109; and Cockerell, 109–10; and contemporary writers, 110, 111; conceals her early history, 112; fulfils her material ambitions, 114–15, 116; the "Max Gate look", 115, 120; living in London, 115–16; relationship with Barrie, 116–20; and Sassoon, 120; entertains American academics, 121; death of, 129; ignored by T.H.'s biographers, 131

—Character 131; class consciousness, 6, 22, 37, 42, 45, 71, 116; devotion to duty, 15; lacking in confidence, 16, 111; sensitivity and nervousness, 18, 51, 70, 80, 109; melancholy, 28, 66; discipline, 45; tact, 54; sympathy, 65; generosity, 66, 80, 113–14, 122; impulsiveness, 82; pessimism, 82; affection, 83; empathy with animals, 84; conscientiousness, 100; depressions, 103; truthfulness, 108; warm-heartedness, 122; love of children, 124; commonsense and kindness, 133

—Family, 82–3; and her father, 12, 21, 129; nurses her mother, 38; sends Margaret to college, 66; at her death, 129

—Participation in local affairs: Borough Magistrate, 100, 123–5; Dorset General Hospital, 122–3; Mill Street Housing Society, 125–8

—"Scribbling woman": aspiring writer, 23, 24, 32, 47, 84–5; writes for *Enfield*

Observer, 26; her literary style, 26, 84; learns journalist's craft, 27; journalist, 34–7, 52, 63; commissioned by Oxford University Press, 63; her verse, 63, 84–5; reviews for *The Sphere*, 86; abandons writing, 90

— Teaching: pupil–teacher, 13–14, 15; in her father's school, 16, 18–19, 22, 32; end of teaching career, 33

— Works: *The Apotheosis of the Minx*, 32; *Blue Jimmy*, 63; *A Book of Baby Beasts*, 63; *A Book of Baby Birds*, 63; *A Book of Baby Pets*, 85; *In Lucy's Garden*, 27, 47, 66–7

— Henry, T.H.'s brother, 100; F.H. and, 59, 72; T.H. and, 69; at Hardy's wedding, 73; and T.H.'s burial, 107; and Hardy Memorial, 109; his prosperity, 113

— Kate, T.H.'s sister, 50, 113; F.H. and, 59, 72, 82; chaperones F.H. and T.H., 64, 84; Emma Hardy and, 70; and T.H.'s burial, 107; and Hardy Memorial, 109

— Mary, T.H.'s sister, F.H. and, 59, 64, 72; death of, 81; and T.H., 86

— Players, 101

— Theresa, T.H.'s cousin, 113–14

— Thomas, memorial for, 3, 107; Maugham on, 7; Hyatt's anthology of, 28–9; at sixty-seven, 30; agnostic, 30, 52, 105; and *The Apotheosis of the Minx*, 33; and women's clothes, 36; May Sinclair on, 46; and Clodd, 47, 57; Clodd's guest with F.H. at Aldeburgh, 49–51, 63; F.H.'s sister and nephew meet, 52; F.H.'s article for *Evening Standard* on, 52–3, 132; and Emma Hardy, 55, 56, 59, 67, 69, 71, 80, 122; and death of his cat, 57; Strang to draw, 49; and Florence Henniker, 61, 65; F.H. on Lilian Gifford's opinion of, 68; his hatred of journalists, 69; importance of his past to, 70; visits Dugdales, 72; structural changes at Max Gate, 77; his obsession with Emma after her death, 77, 83, 86, 92, 93, 108; attitude to 1914 War, 79; and Mrs. Hanbury, 80–81; and Clodd's memoirs, 82; a recluse, 85; and Shorter, 86–7, 101; his *Life*, 88–90, 91, 99, 108, 111–12; homage to, 95–6; health, 97, 104; and dramatization of *The Return of the Native*, 101; and Florence Bugler, 101, 102–3; death of, 106; burial arrangements, 107; his estate, 113; proposed publication of his letters, 120; and magistracy, 123; Maugham and, 131–3

— Character: hypochondria, 57, 61; self-absorption, 57; stinginess, 57, 78, 80, 83, 113, 122; luxuriating in misery, 57; selfishness, 79; inhospitality, 80; susceptibility to young women, 80, 100, 101; mother-fixation, 117

— and F.H.: "biography" of, 3, 4, 88–90, 91, 99, 107–9, 110–12; her devotion, 5, 45, 68; her first introduction to, 28; help with *The Dynasts*, 29, 30; gives her presents, 30; relationship between, 31–2, 33, 47, 51, 83, 97–8; and her career as journalist, 34, 37, 52, 63; and her health, 33, 47, 49, 63, 80, 99–100; F.H. his secretary, 46, 52, 87; her changing attitude to, 53, 54; meetings between, 61, 64; and her Detmold books, 63; after Emma's death, 68–9; gossip about relationship between, 69; F.H. on, 70, 83; site for her grave, 70; and marriage, 71; the issue forced, 72; their wedding, 73; his interest in young women, 80–81, 100, 101, 103; F.H. on their marriage, 81; her resentment against, 83; F.H. his amanuensis, 87; his dependence on her, 87, 97, 99; her protective solicitude for him, 103–4, 106; his death, 106, 107; F.H. his trustee, 109, 110; his provision for her, 113; F.H. and his poetry, 133–4

— Works: dramatic adaptations, *The Return of the Native*, 101; *The Trumpet Major*, 67; epic drama, *The Dynasts*, 29, 30, 53, 79, 96; novels, *The Mayor of Casterbridge*, 125; *A Pair of Blue Eyes*, 29; *Tess of the d'Urbervilles*, 102; opera, *Tess of the d'Urbervilles*, 49; poems, *After the visit*, 55; *Had You Wept*, 55; *In Her Precincts*, 81; *In the Street*, 68; *The Ivy Wife*, 29; *In a Eweleaze near Weatherbury*, 29; *On the Departure Platform*, 30–31; *To Shakespeare After Three Hundred Years*, 87; *Zermatt: to the Matterhorn*, 51; short story, *Old Mrs. Chundle*, 111; volumes of poetry, *Moments of Vision*, 95, *Poems of 1912–1913*, 69, *Satires of Circumstance*, 79

Harrison, Jane, 38

Henniker, Florence, 29, 72, 105; F.H. on, 36, 61; T.H. on, 60–61; F.H.'s post with, 60–61; character, 61; and death of her husband, 65; High Churchwoman, 65; and F.H.'s compromising situation, 69–70; T.H.'s letters to, 71, 73, 120; death of, 97

— General, 61, 65

Hoare, Alda, Lady, 38, 77, 91; invited to Max Gate, 6; gifts of game, 79; F.H. corresponds with, 91, 92; and Emma Hardy, 91–2

Hodder and Stoughton, 84

Hodson, G. H., 21

— W. S. R., 21

Hyatt, Alfred, 32, 72, 104; history, health, dress, 25–6; collaborates with F.H. on *Enfield Observer*, 26; his influence on F.H., 26–7, 36, 67; anthologist, 27, 28–9, 36, 60, 133; relationship with F.H., 28; *The Pocket Thomas Hardy*, 28–9; writes local guide book, 34; F.H.'s devotion to, 36, 51,

Hyatt, Alfred—*contd.*
64; death of, 64; burial of, 65; *From a Middlesex Garden*, 66
—Elizabeth, 25

Ilchester, Lady, 5, 77, 131
Irving, Henry, 40
—Laurence, 43

James, Henry, 5
Jeune, Lady, 38, 77, 80, 91, 131
Johnson, Samuel, 34
Jones, Mrs. Doyle, 102
Jones, Henry Arthur, 131

Keats, John, 12, 61, 96

Lawrence, D. H., 23
—T. E., 96, 107, 110, 111, 113
Lemperly, Paul, 115
Londonderry, Lady, 36
Lucas, Mrs. E. V., 118
Lyceum Club, 46, 53, 54

MacCarthy, Desmond, 111
Macmillan, Daniel, 110
—Sir Frederick, 32, 90
Marshall, Archibald, 32
Maugham, William Somerset, *Cakes and Ale*, 3–7, 112, 131–3; on T.H., 7
Max Gate, pilgrims to, 3; Maugham ridicules, 5–6; F.H. stays at, 54, 55, 67, 68; furnishings, 56; cats at, 67; Emma Hardy's death at, 67; F.H. takes charge, 68; F.H. on life at, 68, 69; F.H. makes changes, 77; primitive conditions at, 86, 99; visitors to, 95, 96–7, 100, 104, 121; foundations, 95; social and literary centre, 97; improved amenities at, 97; Hardy Players at, 101; Emma's effects destroyed at, 109; dining-room a memorial to T.H., 112; Lady Cynthia Asquith at, 115.
Meredith, George, 50
Mill Street Housing Society, 125–8, 129
Milnes, Richard Monckton, 1st Baron Houghton, 61
Moore, George, 40, 42, 43
Motley, John Lothrop, 91
Murry, John Middleton, 96

Nesbit, E., 26

O'Rourke, Miss, 99
Ouida, 13
Owen, Rebekah, 35, 91, 92, 103
Oxford University Press, 63, 121

Parrish, G. T., 42
Pollard, A. W., 32
Potter Beatrix, 26

Priestley, J. B., 4
Punch, 91

Queen's College, Oxford, 109
Quiller-Couch, Sir Arthur, 77, 111
—Lady, 77

Reid, Jean, 35
—Whitlaw, 35
Richardson, Ethel, *see* Dugdale, Ethel
Riggs, Jane, 79, 93
"Rita", 46

Salisbury, Marchioness of, 15
Sassoon, Siegfried, 5, 96, 104; visits Max Gate, 95; and F.H., 110, 120, 132
Scott, Lady, 118
Senior, Nassau, 14–15
Shaw, George Bernard, 117–18
Sheridan, Mary, 91
Shipton, Dick, 114, 116, 129
Shorter, Annie Doris, 100, 101
—Clement, 59; editor of *The Sphere*, 34; and F.H., 34–5, 86; and Hyatt's anthology, 36; Clodd's guest, 51; and Father Dawson, 65; and F.H.'s compromising situation, 69–70; irritates T.H., 70; T.H.'s resentment of, 86–7; makes a second marriage, 100–101
Sigerson, Dora (Mrs. Clement Shorter), 54, 86; T.H.'s attitude to, 34; her poem in Hyatt's anthology, 36; and F.H.'s post with Lady Stoker, 39; Clodd's guest, 51; and Father Dawson, 65; and F.H.'s compromising situation, 69–70
—Dr. George, 39
Sinclair, May, 31, 46
Society of Authors, 95
Somerset, Miss Gwendolen, 10
Sparks, Tryphena, T.H.'s cousin, 29
Sphere, The, 34, 35, 36, 38, 59, 86
Stevenson, R. L., 13
Stinsford, 3, 4–5, 70, 129
Stoker, Bram, 40, 43, 66
—Lady (Emily), 72; F.H. companion to, 39–40; her illness, 40, 43; death of, 43, 57
—Sir Thornley, 61, 72, 105; Dublin surgeon, 39; his popularity, 40, 66; character, 40, 60; his influence on F.H., 40–42, 123; his generosity and kindliness, 42–3; baronet, 43; and his wife, 43, 57; gives F.H. a ring, 60; illness and death of, 65–6; his legacy to F.H., 66
Stopes, Marie, 31
Strang, William, 59
Swinburne, Algernon Charles, 51, 61
Syrett, Netta, 46

Taylor, A. J. P., 127
—Alicia, F.H.'s aunt, 10

Tennyson, Alfred, Lord, 26
Thackeray, William Makepeace, 61
Thiers, Louis Adolphe, 61
Times, The, 22, 109, 126, 127
Titterington, Nellie, 71, 106, 116, 117, 122
Tomlinson, H. M., 110, 129
—Mrs. H. M., 4, 129
Trevelyan, G. M., 32

Wales, Edward, Prince of, *later* Duke of Windsor, 97
Walpole, Sir Hugh, 111, 132
Ward, Hon. John, 35
Webb, Betty, 40, 43, 66

Weber, Carl J., 121
Wells, H. G., 95
Wessex, the Hardys' terrier, 72, 85, 96, 97, 104
West, Rebecca, 95
Westminster Abbey, 3, 107
Whymper, Edward, 51
—Mrs. Edward, 51
Wise, T. J., 86
Womens' suffrage, 35, 59
Woolf, Virginia, 32

Yearsley, Louisa, 93, 99, 100, 109
—Macleod, 80, 86, 93, 99, 100
Young, Sir E. Hilton, 127